Promoting Equitable Math Instruction: Exploring Elementary Teachers' Stories presents cases reflecting real-world and classroom contexts that mathematics teachers often face. I appreciate that the accompanying reflection questions encourage critical examination of teaching practices, communication, and engagement with families. I believe that the cases support professional dialogue, helping individual teachers or teams of teachers to deepen their understanding of equitable mathematics teaching.
  Dr. Robert Q. Berry, *Past President of the National Council of Teachers of Mathematics (2018–2020)*

Promoting Equitable Math Instruction: Exploring Elementary Teachers' Stories is an essential read for math teachers, school administrators, and special education and intervention specialists aiming to understand and tackle inequity in math classrooms. The phrase, "I'm not a math person" is all too common, reflecting how students' mathematical identities are shaped early on. Elementary teachers play a crucial role in this development. This book provides a framework to counter deficit thinking and recognize how even well-intentioned math practices can inadvertently harm students' identities. Through relatable case studies, the book presents scenarios many educators have likely encountered, allowing readers to examine them from an observer's perspective. The inclusion of noticing frameworks encourages critical reflection, helping readers identify and explore alternative behaviors to address the inequities observed in the case studies. Presenting the points for consideration at the end of the book, rather than at the end of each case, provides readers the space to make their own observations and arrive at their own learning, while still offering guidance toward more equitable, inclusive, and asset-based math teaching practices. The engaging narratives make it a quick yet impactful read, offering valuable insights for promoting equity in math education. This book serves as an excellent professional development resource for administrators seeking to engage their teachers in deep, reflective dialogue that will lead to improved academic, social-emotional, and equitable outcomes for their schools.
  Dr. Rachael Mahmood, *2024 Illinois Teacher of the Year, Consultant at Equity Teacher Leader*

Promoting Equitable Math Instruction: Exploring Elementary Teachers' Stories is a powerful and essential guide that challenges educators to uncover the often-overlooked barriers to student belonging and success. Its powerful scenarios and reflective questions push us beyond judgment, urging a deep examination of our own practices and the systems we uphold.

Kim Broomer, *2025 Washington State Teacher of the Year*

As a National Board Certified teacher in a Title I elementary school, I found this book to be both affirming and eye-opening. The case studies presented were deeply relatable—some mirrored my own lived experiences in the classroom, while others expanded my understanding of equity in ways I hadn't previously considered. I appreciated the complexity and nuance the authors brought to real-world teaching scenarios, particularly in how race, language, socioeconomic status, and family engagement intersect with math instruction. Even as someone who has served as my school's equity partner and currently participates in a community of practice focused on family engagement, I found myself reexamining some of my own assumptions and decisions. This book is more than a professional read—it's a reflective tool that invites educators into critical self-awareness and growth. I highly recommend it to any teacher, coach, or administrator seeking to deepen their equity work in mathematics.

Kathryn Lee, *National Board Certified Teacher, Pitt County Schools, North Carolina*

Promoting Equitable Math Instruction

Step into K–5 classrooms and examine equitable math instruction. Through authentic cases from current and former math teachers, this book explores the complexities of teaching math in ways that empower every learner. Whether engaging in personal reflection or collaborative professional development, each chapter challenges you to examine your own practice by confronting assumptions, uncovering bias, and reimagining your role as a math teacher or leader.

This book features a collection of 20 cases organized around themes of classroom policies and procedures, communication, instructional pedagogies and tasks, and family and community engagement. Designed for K–5 teachers, instructional coaches, and school leaders, every case includes reflection questions and points for consideration to extend thinking and guide ongoing growth. By exploring both equitable and inequitable teaching practices, this book equips you to recognize how instructional decisions can hinder or support access and success for all students.

Whether you're new to the classroom or a seasoned educator, this book invites you to spark meaningful change. It challenges you to question deficit-based assumptions, reconsider traditional notions of who participates and succeeds in math, and critically reflect on your instructional decisions. With insight and inspiration, this book empowers you to cultivate inclusive math classrooms where every student is valued, supported, and positioned to thrive.

Dr. Monica L. Gonzalez is an Associate Professor of Elementary Mathematics Education at East Carolina University, and a former elementary math teacher and assistant principal.

Dr. Alesia Mickle Moldavan is an Associate Professor of Elementary Mathematics and Science Education at Georgia Southern University, and a former secondary math teacher.

Equity and Social Justice in Education Series

Paul C. Gorski, Series Editor

Routledge's Equity and Social Justice in Education series is a publishing home for books that apply critical and transformative equity and social justice theories to the work of on-the-ground educators. Books in the series describe meaningful solutions to the racism, white supremacy, economic injustice, sexism, heterosexism, transphobia, ableism, neoliberalism, and other oppressive conditions that pervade schools and school districts.

Igniting Real Change for Multilingual Learners
Equity and Advocacy in Action
Carly Spina

Anti-Oppressive Universal Design for Teachers
Building Equitable Classrooms
Diana Ma

Integrating Educator Well-Being, Growth, and Evaluation
Four Foundations for Leaders
Lori Cohen and Elizabeth Denevi

Humanizing Pedagogies with Multilingual Learners
Transforming Teaching in Content Areas
Kara Mitchell Viesca and Nancy L. Commins

From Empathy to Action
Empowering K-6 Students to Create Change Through Reading, Writing, and Research
Chris Hass, Katie Kelly, and Lester Laminack

Promoting Equitable Math Instruction
Exploring Elementary Teachers' Stories
Monica L. Gonzalez and Alesia Mickle Moldavan

Promoting Equitable Math Instruction

Exploring Elementary Teachers' Stories

Monica L. Gonzalez and Alesia Mickle Moldavan

NEW YORK AND LONDON

Cover image: Getty Images

First published 2026
by Routledge
605 Third Avenue, New York, NY 10158

and by Routledge
4 Park Square, Milton Park, Abingdon, Oxon, OX14 4RN

Routledge is an imprint of the Taylor & Francis Group, an informa business

© 2026 Monica L. Gonzalez and Alesia Mickle Moldavan

The right of Monica L. Gonzalez and Alesia Mickle Moldavan to be identified as authors of this work has been asserted in accordance with sections 77 and 78 of the Copyright, Designs and Patents Act 1988.

All rights reserved. No part of this book may be reprinted or reproduced or utilised in any form or by any electronic, mechanical, or other means, now known or hereafter invented, including photocopying and recording, or in any information storage or retrieval system, without permission in writing from the publishers.

Trademark notice: Product or corporate names may be trademarks or registered trademarks, and are used only for identification and explanation without intent to infringe.

ISBN: 978-1-032-98741-5 (pbk)
ISBN: 978-1-003-60027-5 (ebk)

DOI: 10.4324/9781003600275

Typeset in Palatino
by SPi Technologies India Pvt Ltd (Straive)

Contents

Acknowledgments x
Meet the Authors xii
Foreword xiv
Preface xviii

1 Introduction 1
    Cases for Elementary Math Teacher Professional Learning 5
    How to Use This Book 9

2 Analyzing Cases Using Anti-Deficit Noticing of Math Teaching 10
    Setting the Stage: What Does Equity Look Like in Math Classrooms? 11
    What Does It Mean to Notice? Introducing Noticing Frameworks 16
    A Framework for Challenging Deficit Thinking in Math Education 17
    Moving Forward to Build a Culture of Anti Deficit Noticing 19

3 Cases About Math Classroom Community Norms, Policies, and Procedures 24
    Case 3.1 First-Year Classroom Management 27
    Case 3.2 Differing Perspectives on Teaching Math Word Problems 30
    Case 3.3 Managing Manipulatives to Avoid Mishap 34
    Case 3.4 One Teacher's Push for Inclusive Policies Beyond the Classroom 38
    Case 3.5 Identifying Students for the Gifted Program 42

4 Cases About Communication in Math Classrooms 45

Case 4.1 Verbal and Nonverbal Communication 48

Case 4.2 Problems with Small Groups 51

Case 4.3 Reframing and Valuing Student Voice 54

Case 4.4 Math Is a Universal Language? 56

Case 4.5 Building Math Confidence Through Asset-Based
Language 61

5 Cases About Math Instructional Pedagogies and Tasks 64

Case 5.1 Gender and Binary Story Problems 67

Case 5.2 Using Technology to Practice Place Value 70

Case 5.3 Overcoming Roadblocks in a "Race to Mastery" 73

Case 5.4 Comparing Fractions in Safe Spaces with
Number Talks 77

Case 5.5 Stuck in the Script 81

6 Cases About Engaging Families and Communities in Math 84

Case 6.1 Supporting Multilingual Families with
Math Content 87

Case 6.2 Advocating Access to Extracurricular
Math Activities 90

Case 6.3 Navigating Family Help with Homework 93

Case 6.4 Exploring Community Partnerships to Enhance
Math Applications 97

Case 6.5 Flea Market Experience 100

7 Points for Consideration 103

Case 3.1 First-Year Classroom Management 105

Case 3.2 Differing Perspectives on Teaching Math Word
Problems 107

Case 3.3 Managing Manipulatives to Avoid Mishap 110

Case 3.4 One Teacher's Push for Inclusive Policies Beyond the
    Classroom...113
Case 3.5 Identifying Students for the Gifted Program...........116
Case 4.1 Verbal and Nonverbal Communication...................119
Case 4.2 Problems with Small Groups 121
Case 4.3 Reframing and Valuing Student Voice 123
Case 4.4 Math Is a Universal Language? 125
Case 4.5 Building Math Confidence Through Asset-Based
    Language 128
Case 5.1 Gender and Binary Story Problems.....................132
Case 5.2 Using Technology to Practice Place Value 135
Case 5.3 Overcoming Roadblocks in a "Race to Mastery".........139
Case 5.4 Comparing Fractions in Safe Spaces with
    Number Talks..141
Case 5.5 Stuck in the Script 144
Case 6.1 Supporting Multilingual Families with
    Math Content 148
Case 6.2 Advocating Access to Extracurricular
    Math Activities 150
Case 6.3 Navigating Family Help with Homework 152
Case 6.4 Exploring Community Partnerships to Enhance
    Math Applications...154
Case 6.5 Flea Market Experience 156

Appendix: Process for Analyzing Cases Using
Anti-Deficit Noticing *159*
References *160*

Acknowledgments

Critical friends are trusted individuals who provide constructive feedback and insights to help improve someone's thinking or work. We used many critical friends throughout the multiple drafts of this book. We, just like everyone else, need critical friends to check our biases about math instruction and how the teachers and students are presented in the stories. These people provided critical feedback and perspectives based on their experience and research of math teaching to help make the cases in this book relatable for you.

We would like to express our sincere appreciation to the elementary teachers, teacher leaders, and math teacher educators who helped support the writing of this book. Some of those people are Aliza Robinson, Clark County School District; Amy Dunning; Ana Floyd, Asheboro City Schools; Anne Cawley, Cal Poly Pomona; Bailey Nafziger, Georgia Southern University; Brette Garner, University of Denver; Carrie Wilkerson Lee, East Carolina University; Daniel Greco, Wake County Public School System; Erin Smith, University of Nevada Las Vegas; Jameesa Walker, Benhaven Elementary School; Jennifer Ward, Kennesaw State University; Joseph DiNapoli, Montclair State University; Katherine Baker, Elon University; Kendra N. Bledsoe, Guilford County Schools; Robyn K. Pinilla, the University of Texas at El Paso; and Sarah Remery. There were many more, behind the scenes, who shared their stories and insights, which were instrumental to creating this book. We are truly grateful for your willingness to present these stories in an authentic and meaningful way.

We would also like to acknowledge Paul Gorski, whose unwavering commitment to equity and social justice in education continues to be a guiding force for many. We are deeply honored and humbled by the opportunity to include our work in the *Equity and Social Justice in Education* series. This series has served as a platform for critical dialogue, empowering teachers, scholars, and advocates to confront the complexities of inequity and push for transformative justice.

Finally, we are deeply grateful to our family and friends for their unwavering love, patience, and reassurance throughout this journey. Your constant support, whether through thoughtful insights, warm meals, or encouraging words, sustained us in ways we will never forget. We truly could not have done this without you, and we promise to stop talking about "the book" until our next one!

Meet the Authors

 **Monica L. Gonzalez**, PhD, is an Associate Professor of Elementary Mathematics Education at East Carolina University, where she educates and mentors both pre-service and in-service teachers. Her earlier experiences as an elementary teacher and assistant principal in a diverse Title I school continue to shape her commitment to equitable mathematics teaching. In her university teaching, she uses case-based instruction to help future teachers critically examine their beliefs about students, mathematics learning, and mathematics instruction.

Dr. Gonzalez's work centers on developing compassionate educators who are committed to understanding their students and engaging them in high-quality, equitable mathematics experiences. She has published research on the use of case-based instruction to uncover and confront bias in mathematics teaching and learning, and she integrates practice-based teacher education to support the enactment of equitable mathematics teaching. Her research examines how mathematics teacher educators design learning experiences that support critical reflection, courageous conversations, and intentional planning for justice-oriented mathematics instruction. Dr. Gonzalez regularly presents her work at national and international conferences and is dedicated to building a community of educators who prioritize equity, empathy, and excellence in mathematics classrooms.

Alesia Mickle Moldavan, PhD, is an Associate Professor of Elementary Mathematics and Science Education in the College of Education at Georgia Southern University, where she teaches mathematics and science methods courses to pre-service and in-service teachers. Drawing on her experiences teaching in diverse Title I secondary schools, facilitating  elementary STEM enrichment programs, and supervising K–12 teachers, she brings a wealth of practical and pedagogical experience to her role. Her instruction cultivates meaningful learning experiences by integrating culturally responsive strategies and preparing teachers to identify students' strengths and assets, nurture positive STEM identities, and serve as ethical advocates for all learners.

Dr. Moldavan is extensively published, with contributions to over 25 peer-reviewed journals and authorship of chapters in more than 10 books. Her research focuses on equitable and culturally responsive teaching practices, along with the purposeful integration of digital technologies in teacher education to enhance accessibility and inclusivity. Grounded in a strong commitment to social justice, her scholarship interrogates the impact of systemic inequities on educational outcomes and explores transformative strategies to challenge and disrupt those narratives. Her recent work highlights the design and implementation of innovative curricula and instructional approaches in teacher education that elevate cultural awareness, critically address equity issues, and advance justice-oriented STEM education. By empowering teachers with the tools to recognize and address social injustices in schools, her research fosters the development of socially conscious teachers prepared to lead change within and beyond their classrooms.

Foreword

In 25 years helping educators develop the knowledge and skills required to create and sustain equitable schools—what I call *equity literacy*—I've come to recognize three commitments as the profoundest indications of equity growth. A lot of people, perhaps *most* people, working in schools have some level of general equity knowledge, whether they choose to apply it or not. Most of us, I tend to presume, want each student to succeed. Most of us provide individual supports for students who need them if we know they need them. Most of us appreciate diversity. Some of us don't, of course, and I invite those educators to find a different line of work, far away from children.

For the rest of us, the trouble is that equity requires something more than appreciating diversity, something more than individual-level support. Wanting each student to succeed is an important minimum standard of commitment. But wanting is not understanding or doing. Wanting is not an equity action. The deeper question than *To what extent do I want to provide equity for students?* is *How deeply do I understand the conditions that undermine equity in my spheres of influence?* and *To what extent am I willing and prepared to transform those conditions?*

Our first commitment, then, must be to critical self-reflection. This is our *ideological* commitment. Too much damage is done in schools by people who are well-intended, but unaware of how common, troubling belief systems misdirect good intentions into inequitable policies and practices. In my experience, the most devastating ideological culprit is *deficit ideology*, the belief that educational disparities are primarily the results of supposed deficiencies in students and families of color, students and families experiencing poverty, and other students and families who bear the brunt of injustice in and out of schools. Because deficit ideology obscures the *actual* root causes of disparities—the unjust distribution of access and opportunity, for example—it inevitably leads us to bad solutions that often are just as inequitable as the problems we are trying to solve.

For example, deficit ideology is the set of beliefs that has schools trying to shrink racial discipline disparities by adjusting the behaviors, attitudes, and mindsets of students of color while ignoring the primary cause of the disparities: racial bias in how adults in schools interpret and respond to behaviors depending on the racial identities of students. These beliefs and actions are incompatible with equity. So, we should practice wiggling ourselves free from it and embracing an equity-driven ideology instead.

Our second commitment, in essence, is to strengthen our abilities to recognize even the subtlest, most unintentional ways racism, heterosexism, ableism, and other forms of injustice are operating around us. Subtle and unintentional inequity has the same impact as obvious and intentional inequity. It can have an even deeper impact, actually, because of how insidious it tends to be, and how protected from critical view. It's the policy or practice that looks equal on paper but has inequitable impact, for example, like tardy or homework policies. If we can't or won't ferret out these policies and practices, we simply can't say we're committed to equity.

Our third commitment involves learning how to transition from mitigative to transformative responses to inequity. In equity literacy parlance, we distinguish between *responding to* and *redressing* inequity. Responding is what we do in the moment, in real time. It's usually a mitigation. We adjust how we apply the tardy or homework policy; we interrupt a heterosexist comment; we engage colleagues in a conversation about the deficit view they're embracing. These are important equity moves. But they're only partial equity moves.

The transformative move requires that we do a bit of equity excavating and determine root causes. What sorts of misunderstandings landed us on that inequitable homework policy? How have so many people around us bought into those deficit views, and how are those views supported by institutional culture and practice? If we can push ourselves to this level of curiosity and then direct that curiosity into deeper levels of action, we make ourselves more formidable equity architects.

I've used many tools and pedagogies to help myself and fellow educators strengthen these commitments. But the case study method has been the most potent of these tools and pedagogies. Well-conceived and just-layered-enough case scenarios—the kind with which Monica L. Gonzalez and Alesia Mickle Moldavan filled this book—can provide transformative learning moments. Since Seema Pothini and I wrote the original edition of *Case Studies on Diversity and Social Justice Education* in 2013, many people have sent me sample cases they've written for various purposes. By a very big margin, though, the cases in this book are the most compelling, most intricate, and most relatable I've read. They're not just written; they're *crafted*. I'm excited for you to dive into them.

The authors offer a framework and approach for reading and reflecting on the cases. I just want to encourage you, the reader, to remember the three commitments. It can be easy to read a scenario about something happening in somebody else's classroom, somebody else's school, and distance ourselves from it. But your best learning will happen if you put yourselves in the proverbial shoes of the educators in the cases. Monica and Alesia offer many powerful reflection questions to help you do this. Try not to respond reactively. Instead wonder, imagine, and reflect. Sit with the hard ideological questions. This is your first challenge.

Secondly, use these cases as an opportunity to fortify your *recognizing*. Remember that most of us do well recognizing the kinds of inequity we experience, but most of us struggle to recognize the kinds of inequity that afford us some level of privilege and protection. Every case study has big, obvious circumstances most of us will be able to point out readily as bias or inequity. The best fortifying happens when we dig beneath the surface and examine the subtler stuff. The cases in this book were designed masterfully in this regard. Take your time and examine all the layers. This is the best way to build your equity literacy.

Finally, practice that shifts from mitigating to transforming. Ask yourself, *What would I do in this moment if I was present and observing this scenario happening? What questions would I ask? What actions would I take?* Then, dig deeper. *What are the conditions that underlie what's happening in this scenario? What are the longer-term changes for which I would advocate to address the root causes of the bias or inequity operating here?*

Herein lies the beauty of these case studies, the beauty of this book: When we practice embracing meaningful equity commitments using the sorts of cases you are about to read, we prepare ourselves to apply those commitments in our own classrooms and schools. They become a kind of literacy—a kind of *equity* literacy. If we practice enough, we make equity our natural response, a literal sort of literacy.

With this goal in mind, I urge you to maximize the opportunity Monica and Alesia are providing us. Engage with intention. Reflect deeply. Practice attentively. And grow.

—Paul Gorski, coauthor with Seema Pothini of
Case Studies on Diversity and Social Justice Education

Preface

As former classroom teachers and now teacher educators, teachers' stories have been at the center of our professional growth. When we first started exploring what equity means in education, it wasn't just theories or research that made it click for us. It was the real, everyday classroom stories that challenged us to reflect on our own biases and rethink the way we approached teaching through a critical, asset-based lens. Books like *Case Studies on Diversity and Social Justice Education* (Gorski & Pothini, 2024) and *A Casebook for Exploring Diversity* (Redman & Redman, 2011) gave us powerful examples of teachers wrestling with equity and diversity issues across different grade levels. But when we brought these cases into our elementary math education courses, we kept hearing the same question: "How does this apply to teaching elementary math?"

That question got us thinking. We realized that while equity in education is a broad and important topic, elementary math classrooms have their own unique equity challenges. Elementary teachers need to consider their individual students and their students' emerging math identities that will develop through the instructional decisions teachers make every day. So, we started writing our own cases, drawing from our experiences teaching and the stories other teachers shared with us, focusing specifically on what equity looks like in elementary math. As we shared these cases with colleagues, they encouraged us to take them further and create a resource that would help even more teachers engage in critical reflection about what it truly means to teach math equitably. That's how this book came to be, born out of the real questions, struggles, and insights of teachers just like you.

What This Book is About and How It Can Support Your Teaching

As teachers, we make hundreds of decisions every day, some big and some small, but all with the potential to shape how students experience and understand math. Sometimes, these decisions happen so quickly that we don't even realize the patterns in our thinking or the underlying assumptions guiding our choices. That's where this book comes in. The purpose of this book is to support professional growth by helping you notice equitable and inequitable math teaching that can then be connected to math teaching practices and make intentional connections to your own classroom practice.

The book consists of real-world cases that demonstrate the complexity of teaching elementary math. These cases illustrate the everyday moments when teachers' decisions about instruction, questioning, grouping, participation, assessment, and communication with families affect not only students' learning but also their confidence and identity as math thinkers in kindergarten through fifth grade. We don't just present these cases for discussion; we provide a structured approach to analyzing them through an anti-deficit lens, helping you move beyond traditional narratives of student "gaps" or struggles and instead empower you as the teacher to recognize the strengths, assets, and potential in every child.

At the end of each case, you'll find reflection questions designed to help you engage deeply with the stories, draw on your own experiences, and reflect on the impact of instructional decision-making. We also provide some points for consideration to help broaden your perspective and push your thinking in new directions. The cases have been workshopped with the math education community to ensure they reflect the diverse realities of students, families, and teachers in ways that feel relatable and relevant to elementary teachers. Our hope is that as you work through these cases, you'll begin to see your own teaching through a new lens that challenges deficit thinking, amplifies student strengths, and builds more inclusive, empowering math experiences for all learners.

Who This Book is for and How You Can Use It

This book is for elementary teachers, and those who support them, who care deeply about their students and want to create more equitable math classrooms. We know that teaching math is about more than just numbers and procedures; it's about helping every student see themselves as a capable, confident math thinker. But achieving that requires more than just good intentions. It calls for a willingness to see classroom moments from different perspectives, especially from the student's point of view, and to reflect on how our instructional decisions shape students' experiences.

Equitable math teaching is not about having all of the answers. It's about being open to questioning, learning, and growing. The cases in this book provide elementary teachers with opportunities to practice reframing what they notice about students, students' interactions, and the math content. By analyzing these cases through an anti-deficit lens, you'll have the chance to practice shifting your perspective, moving away from traditional narratives of struggle or ability and toward recognizing the strengths and potential in all students.

You can engage with this book in whatever way best supports your growth. If you prefer personal reflection, you might read through the cases on your own, journaling your thoughts and considering how they apply to your own teaching. If you thrive on discussion and collaboration, you might choose to read the book with colleagues, Whether you are in a professional learning community, a teacher study group, or a teacher education methods course, you can exchange insights and challenge each other's thinking. For teacher educators, instructional coaches, or school leaders, these cases can serve as powerful tools for facilitating critical conversations around equitable math teaching, offering a structured way to unpack complex classroom moments and explore alternative approaches. However you choose to use this book, our hope is that it sparks reflection, deepens your understanding of equity in math teaching, and helps you take meaningful steps toward creating a more just and inclusive learning environment for your students.

The Book's Organization

Equitable math teaching is complex and multifaceted. It requires teachers to attend to their students' individual identities, the ways students interact with one another, and the math content itself. Creating an equitable math classroom isn't just about delivering well-structured lessons, It's about noticing the nuances of how students experience math, the barriers they may face, and the opportunities we create (or unintentionally limit) through our teaching choices.

This book is not a collection of lesson plans, nor is it designed to provide direct instruction on broader equity topics like racism, sexism, ableism, language bias, and other systemic issues. Instead, it offers real-world cases based on the experiences of elementary teachers, providing a space for you to practice noticing issues related to equity in math teaching and develop strategies for responding to similar situations. These cases are meant to help you engage in deep reflection, refine your noticing skills, and build confidence in making more equitable instructional decisions.

The book is organized so that you can navigate it in a way that best suits your needs. Chapter 1 lays the foundation by defining equitable math teaching and discussing the role of math teachers in elementary schools. Since analyzing cases through an anti-deficit lens is crucial, Chapter 2 introduces frameworks for doing just that. The chapter helps teachers move beyond traditional deficit-based thinking and instead recognize the strengths and potential in all students.

The heart of the book lies in Chapters 3 through 6, which present a series of cases centered on key aspects of math teaching. These chapters focus on the following themes:

- ♦ Classroom community norms, policies, and procedures—examining how classroom community norms, routines, and expectations impact student engagement and access to learning math.
- ♦ Communication—considering how teacher language, student discourse, and feedback shape math identities.

- Instructional pedagogies and tasks—analyzing the ways in which math tasks and teaching strategies create opportunities (or barriers) for different learners.
- Family and community engagement—reflecting on the role of families and communities in shaping students' experiences with math.

These chapters do not need to be read in order, nor do you need to read an entire chapter to engage in critical reflection. You can select chapters or individual cases based on the aspects of math teaching that resonate most with your experiences, questions, or challenges as a starting point. Each case includes reflection questions to guide deeper exploration of the equity issues presented.

Finally, Chapter 7 brings everything together, offering points for consideration that help teachers take actionable steps toward more equitable math teaching while critically evaluating the broader implications of how inequities negatively impact students. We believe that all teachers, regardless of experience level, can continue to learn, reflect, and refine their teaching practice. Ultimately, our goal is to help you develop the noticing skills, mindset, and confidence needed to create a math classroom where every student is seen, valued, and empowered as a doer of math.

1

Introduction

"You would not believe the email I just received from a parent," Mr. Turner said to Mr. Morris after school. Mr. Turner and Mr. Morris are both fifth-grade math teachers at an elementary school. Mr. Turner is in his second year of teaching, and Mr. Morris has taught fifth-grade math for seven years. Mr. Turner continued his story by saying, "The mom is upset because Deon told her that I shut him down and won't let him ask questions in class. Can you believe that?"

Mr. Morris asked, "Do you let Deon ask questions?"

Mr. Turner looked at him, surprised and a little offended, before replying, "Of course! I let all my students ask questions!"

Mr. Morris calmly stated, "I'm just wondering why Deon would have made that comment to his mom. He isn't the type of kid who would typically complain about his teachers. Tell me what's happening with Deon in class. Maybe he's misinterpreting something."

Mr. Turner took a deep breath and replied, "I let all my students ask questions, but Deon interrupts me constantly to ask questions instead of just listening to what I'm saying. It's disrupting the rest of the class, so I told him that he needs to listen to me instead of interrupting.

> I will probably answer his questions if he just listens. He's just so disrespectful."
>
> Mr. Morris asked, "When does this usually happen?"
>
> Mr. Turner looked confused and replied, "During class."
>
> Mr. Morris rephrased his question and asked, "At what point during the lesson does Deon have the most questions?"
>
> Mr. Turner again looked confused when he said, "When I'm teaching."
>
> Mr. Morris thought for a moment before he said, "I taught Deon's older sister last year, and I got to know their parents pretty well. Their parents teach them to seek clarity when they are unsure and to speak up when they need help. In their family, teachers are held in high respect, and education is something that is taken very seriously. I wonder if Deon's questions are his way of seeking understanding from you and not him purposefully being disrespectful to you."
>
> Mr. Turner took a minute to let Mr. Morris's words wash over him. He thought to himself, *Maybe Mr. Morris has a point*. As he thanked Mr. Morris for talking with him, he began wondering how he should respond to Deon's mom. He knows he should respond soon and probably talk to Deon as well.

Sharing stories of personal experience is a fundamental part of human interactions. You may share stories for many different reasons about the content you teach, your students, or your students' families. Perhaps the purpose of your story sharing is to build empathy with your colleagues to find encouragement and support during challenging situations. You may also choose to share stories to gain perspective and learn from someone else. The beauty of sharing stories with others is that each individual comes with different backgrounds, lived experiences, and perspectives that help to interpret the situations in different ways. Often, it is through sharing these stories that we learn more about our students and how they experience school, which can help us to make equitable teaching decisions and maintain high expectations for all our students.

This book offers you the opportunity to self-reflect and uncover your assumptions and biases through the use of stories. Examining your assumptions and biases about students and math instruction are essential components for enacting equitable math instruction. Biases, whether explicit or implicit, are prevalent in math classrooms. Take, for example, the model minority myth that Asian American students are inherently better at math than other students (Moldavan & Gonzalez, 2023; Shah, 2019). This myth could lead teachers to take actions that highlight the intellectual contributions of Asian American students more often than other students.

On the other hand, research has shown that teachers often view Black and Brown students through a deficit lens, focusing on perceived math shortcomings and deficiencies, which leads to interventions and remediation instead of teachers recognizing their students' math strengths and brilliance (Leonard & Martin, 2013; Louie et al., 2021; Martin et al., 2017). Our perceptions of who we think is "smart" and capable of engaging in rigorous math, which children we choose to center in our math instruction, and the pedagogical strategies we deem appropriate all reflect our implicit biases and assumptions. These beliefs significantly shape our instructional decisions, which can either marginalize students or affirm and elevate them during math learning.

Let's unpack the story of Mr. Turner and Mr. Morris. Did you find yourself wanting to know more details about the situation than what was provided? Maybe you wanted to know more about the student or how Mr. Turner taught his math class. These details were purposefully left out so we could explore how our brains use assumptions to fill in missing information to make sense of the story. Your assumptions could be based on your prior experiences as a teacher, a student, a parent, or a caregiver. You could also base your assumptions on movies you have watched, books you have read, or information that has been shared with you through current events. Your prior experiences and assumptions provide a framing for how you interpret events, like the ones presented in this story, even if you fill in details that were not actually provided to you. Becoming aware of those assumptions is the first step you need to take to critically analyze both equitable and inequitable situations in math classrooms.

Let's examine your assumptions about the student in this case, Deon. The name Deon was chosen intentionally, yet Deon's race was not stated. Did you create an image in your mind of Deon and assign a particular race to him? If so, did you also assign him mannerisms and intentions behind his actions? Maybe the name Deon reminds you of someone you know, and you assigned him similar characteristics in your mind. Let's pretend you know a Black man with the name Deon, so you assumed Deon is a Black child. Black children are often unfairly characterized as being disrespectful and aggressive. If you have heard this type of negative rhetoric and then had it reinforced through the media, you might have assumed malicious intent behind Deon's questions during math class. Those assumptions could lead you to align with Mr. Turner's interpretation of Deon's behavior as motivated disrespect, maybe to gain attention from those around him or deflect from his inadequacies or lack of confidence being "successful" at school. However, you might have personal experiences that are in direct opposition to the negative rhetoric about Black children.

Perhaps you know that Black children are just as respectful and studious as any child, regardless of their race and background. In fact, you might have made an assumption that Mr. Turner was unfairly targeting Deon by telling him not to ask so many questions in class. In this case, your interpretation might have aligned with Mr. Morris, who interpreted Deon's questions as a way of seeking help when he wanted to understand the math content. Interpreting Deon's questions as disrespectful could result in a response that is defensive or provides little patience, which can negatively impact his identity and success with math. However, interpreting Deon's questions as a way of seeking information because he cares about his understanding of the math content could result in a response that is more caring and supportive, recognizing Deon's assets and his math journey. The teacher's interpretation impacts the actions the teacher takes, which will ultimately impact the student's experience in the math classroom.

Maybe you read this case and were not at all concerned with Deon's behavior, but instead, you wanted to know more about Mr. Turner's math instruction. Did you paint a picture in your mind of what Mr. Turner's math lesson was like? If so, what was Mr. Turner doing when he was "teaching?" What were the students doing? Let's now unpack your assumptions about math instruction.

Once again, little information is provided about how Mr. Turner structures his math class. Mr. Turner states that Deon asked many questions while he was teaching, but what does this mean? Maybe your prior experiences as a math student or teaching math have led you to believe that a math teacher's role is to demonstrate and explain how to solve math problems while students silently follow along. If you have these assumptions about math instruction, then your interpretation would lead you to want to change Deon's behavior when he asks questions.

On the other hand, your prior experiences might lead you to believe that students learn math concepts best when they can explore, make connections to prior knowledge, and discuss their ideas with one another. If so, you might have interpreted Mr. Turner's math instruction as teacher-centered and focused on his own problem-solving strategies instead of taking his students' needs into consideration. This interpretation would lead you to want to change how Mr. Turner is structuring his math class instead of changing Deon's behavior.

As you engage with the stories in this book, do so with both an open and critical mind. Reflect on *your* initial reactions and consider *why* you are responding in particular ways. We challenge you to examine your biases as you make a connection between these stories and your own instructional decisions.

Cases for Elementary Math Teacher Professional Learning

Cases are real-life narrative stories that unfold over a period of time (Shulman, 1992). In this book, the cases come from elementary teachers who share their experiences with teaching math, planning lessons, or communicating with families and communities about children's math learning. These stories give a glimpse into the everyday realities of classrooms, including the unique children in them and the thoughtful, sometimes tough, instructional decisions teachers make.

In this book, we use the case method as a tool for uncovering biases, challenging deficit views of children and math, and then reframing the math instructional practices of elementary teachers. The case method uses real-life stories to place the reader in complex classroom dilemmas in which the reader reflects on the instructional decisions of the teachers and the impact those decisions have on the students. Cases allow the reader to be exposed to background information about the setting and learning environment, internal dialogue of teachers and sometimes the students, the math learning goals, and the behaviors and actions of teachers and students in a math classroom setting. Cases also expose the background information about the students, such as their cultural and linguistic backgrounds, learning needs, and prior math experiences and knowledge, which are essential for teachers to consider when making decisions that either challenge or reinforce stereotypes about students engaging in math learning.

As you read the cases in this book, you will take an active role in challenging and possibly changing the narrative that is presented to you. But before you can do that, you first must be aware of your own perspectives and how those perspectives impact students' math identities and math learning.

Attending to Students' Math Identities

Identities are self-perceptions about who we think we are, who we want to become, or who we are not (Aguirre et al., 2024). Identities are diverse and complex and can be rooted in family, religion, culture, race, and gender. You may be thinking of your own identities right now. Your identity could be as a teacher, as a parent, as a friend, as an alumnus from a particular university, and so on. Identities are continuously forming during elementary school, and it is important for elementary teachers to consider their students' developing identities when making instructional decisions. Have you thought about your students' identities and how they see themselves as learners? More specifically, what about how your students see themselves as math learners?

Math identity is the deeply held beliefs students develop about their ability to participate and perform effectively in math contexts and use math in their own lives (Aguirre et al., 2024). Have you ever heard someone say they are not a "math person?" This person has a negative math identity. When students form a negative math identity, they are less willing to persevere during problem-solving, share rough draft math ideas and strategies, or pursue advanced math classes (Rhodes et al., 2023). But what role does the teacher play in the formation of students' math identities?

Power Dynamics in Elementary Math Classrooms

As teachers, we have a lot of power in the classroom. We choose what is taught, how it is taught, whose ideas are publicly shared, and then decide how to grade students' work. Let's examine a couple of common scenarios from math students that exhibit teachers' power.

First, imagine you are a third-grade student who is learning multiplication facts. You know most of them by heart, but your 7s and 8s still take you a while to calculate. Your teacher decides that every week will be a timed multiplication test for the class to test their recall of multiplication facts. Everyone has one minute to complete as many of the multiplication facts as possible, and the first three students who are done get a prize. You know that it's always the same three students who get the prize, so you do not try to be the first one done. In fact, you have never finished the whole test in one minute, so you do not push yourself to try. After many of these timed multiplication tests, you begin to doubt that you even know the multiplication facts that you thought you knew. Now you begin to think of the students who finish first as *good* math students and yourself as a *bad* math student.

In this scenario, the teacher decided on a task that values speed as a way of evaluating students' math understanding. Students who are quick at calculating are seen as good math students, and students who do not complete their time tests begin to internalize a math identity that they are bad at math. However, the teacher could have picked different ways for students to demonstrate the depths of their understanding of the multiplication facts that would have reinforced positive math identities for more students.

In a different scenario, imagine you are a first-grade student who overhears the teacher say, "Ugh! We are in America. They need to learn English!" when your class walks by a group of bilingual students. Now, imagine that multiple languages are spoken in your home. You might feel scared that your teacher will find out about your family, so you decide to be as quiet as possible in class so you do not draw your teacher's attention. This means you do not raise your hand when you have the answer to the math problem, and you never try to be the first or last one done with their math work. Eventually, your math identity becomes one in which you see yourself as having value when you hide your family background. As adults, teachers' words have power, whether those words were meant to be heard or not by their students. In this scenario, the teacher's comments impacted the relationship with the student and how the student felt about themselves as a learner in the class.

Elementary students have little power in their lives. Adults decide when they wake up, go to bed, what they eat, what activities they do, and who their teachers are. Teachers have the power to decide which students sit next to each other, which tasks students engage in, how the classroom is organized, how students' work will be graded, what behavior is acceptable or unacceptable, and so on. All the decisions teachers make on a day-to-day basis demonstrate their power and have direct impacts on students' identities, particularly their math identities.

As elementary teachers, we know you care about your students. But making decisions that build positive math identities for your students will require you to do more than just care about your students. You will need to confront your current assumptions and biases about children, their communities, and math teaching. Then you can explore alternative perspectives that might help you respond to classroom dilemmas in more equitable ways that build positive math identities for all your students.

How to Use This Book

In this book, we offer twenty cases of elementary math teaching that are written from our own experiences in math classrooms or those we have been told by other math teachers. Each case offers a complex classroom dilemma in which a teacher has to make a decision. Some of the outcomes of the teachers' decisions lead to inequities, while other outcomes are more equitable. It is up to you to read and interpret the cases.

However, we want to ensure that you have a way of confronting your assumptions and biases as you read these cases. In Chapter 2, we present the frameworks that guided the writing of the cases and will help you develop a lens for analyzing and critiquing the dilemmas. This chapter is essential for knowing how to approach these cases in productive and meaningful ways.

Chapters 3 through 6 contain cases that are centered around key aspects of math teaching. Each case includes reflection questions to guide deeper explorations and possible alternative points of view on the equity issues. If you are not sure how to answer some of the reflection questions or wish to explore the case in more detail, we encourage you to visit Chapter 7, as it provides additional information about the equity issues. Together, these cases and your reflections can pave the way for more just and inclusive math teaching practices.

2
Analyzing Cases Using Anti-Deficit Noticing of Math Teaching

In this chapter, we'll explore what it means to teach math through an equity-focused lens and why it matters in your classroom. We'll start by looking at the Equity Literacy Framework (Gorski & Pothini, 2024; Gorksi & Swalwell, 2015) alongside Aguirre et al.'s (2024) equity-based practices for math teaching. These ideas help us reflect on our own teaching, recognize the power we have to shape equitable learning spaces, and understand our responsibility in making math accessible and meaningful for all students.

From there, we'll dive into noticing frameworks, which help us become more intentional about what we pay attention to in the classroom, how we interpret what we see, and how we respond. This connects directly to the attending, interpreting, and responding components of the Equity Literacy Framework (Gorski & Pothini, 2024; Gorksi & Swalwell, 2015), sharpening our ability to notice and address inequities in real-time.

To put this all into practice in the math context, we'll introduce the FAIR Framework (Louie et al., 2021), which challenges common deficit-based thinking about students, their math abilities, and their communities. This approach encourages an anti-deficit perspective, meaning we focus on students' strengths rather than perceived shortcomings. By the end of the chapter, you'll have concrete tools to critically analyze classroom interactions, such as those in the following chapters' cases. You'll also be able to leverage these tools to reflect on your teaching decisions and ensure that every student feels valued and capable in their math journey.

Setting the Stage: What Does Equity Look Like in Math Classrooms?

If you were to walk into an equitable math classroom, what would you expect to see? Would it be a place where every student has access to the same materials and resources? Or would it be a space where instruction is thoughtfully adapted to meet students' diverse needs and lived experiences? While access to high-quality math education is critical, equity in math teaching goes beyond simply ensuring that all students receive the same content in the same way. In fact, true equity is not about *sameness*—it's about *fairness* and ensuring that every student has the opportunities and tools they need to thrive mathematically.

Researchers in math education emphasize that equitable teaching requires recognizing and addressing the unique strengths, needs, and experiences of each student, rather than assuming that a one-size-fits-all approach will lead to fair outcomes (Aguirre et al., 2024; Bartell et al., 2017; Gutiérrez, 2009). Gutiérrez (2009) argues that equity in math includes the four domains of access, achievement, identity, and power. Essentially, to achieve equity, we must consider not only students' access to resources to guide high-quality instruction and their academic achievement but also their identities (e.g., culture, values, linguistic resources) and the power dynamics (e.g., agency, voice, student choice) within the learning environment.

Similarly, Aguirre et al. (2024) highlight the importance of using students' cultural knowledge and lived experiences as assets in the math classroom rather than treating them as barriers. When we focus solely on providing the same instruction to all students, we ignore the systemic barriers that disproportionately impact historically marginalized students, including differences in prior opportunities to learn, language backgrounds, and the ways students see themselves as capable mathematicians. A truly equitable approach requires differentiated support, responsive teaching, and a commitment to disrupting practices that privilege certain ways of knowing and doing math over others (Hand, 2012; Langer-Osuna & Esmonde, 2017). By shifting our understanding of equity from sameness to one of fairness, we can better position all students as mathematically competent and valued members of the learning community.

Equity Literacy Framework

To guide us in this shift, we can refer to the Equity Literacy Framework (Gorski & Pothini, 2024; Gorksi & Swalwell, 2015), which is designed to help teachers develop the critical awareness and skills needed to recognize, respond to, and redress inequities in educational settings (see Table 2.1). Rather than focusing on surface-level solutions like celebrating diversity or offering generalized supports, equity literacy encourages teachers to analyze the deeper, systemic factors that create and sustain inequities. This means developing the ability to notice and challenge deficit-based thinking, examine how school structures advantage some students over others, and take meaningful action to create more just learning environments. Within a math classroom, applying equity literacy requires questioning how we assess students' math abilities, how we structure classroom discussions, and how we design learning experiences to be inclusive and affirming. It pushes teachers beyond well-intentioned but insufficient efforts, such as simply incorporating culturally diverse word problems, toward more transformative practices that center students' strengths, identities, and ways of knowing in math. It also encourages teachers to consider their interactions with students and how they assess student understanding. Questions such as *Whose math thinking is valued?* and *How do we position students as capable problem-solvers?* can be asked to guide efforts to create equitable math classrooms.

For example, consider a classroom where a teacher notices that students from multilingual backgrounds are hesitant to participate in math discussions. Using an equity literacy lens, the teacher would look beyond individual student confidence

TABLE 2.1 The Equity Literacy Framework in Math Classrooms

Equity Literacy Skill	Math Classroom Application
Recognizing Inequities	Identifying patterns of participation, achievement gaps, and deficit-based narratives about students' math abilities. *Example*: Noticing that multilingual students are called on less often during class discussions.
Responding to Inequities	Adjusting teaching strategies to challenge inequitable structures. *Example*: Encouraging students to explain math concepts in multiple ways, including using their home languages.
Redressing Inequities	Transforming classroom policies and practices to promote fairness. *Example*: Shifting from speed-based, memorization assessments to tasks that emphasize deep math thinking and conceptual understanding.
Sustaining Equity Efforts	Committing to continuous learning and advocacy in math education. *Example*: Engaging in professional development focused on anti-deficit frameworks and student-centered math teaching.

Note: Adapted from the core components of the Equity Literacy Framework (Gorski & Pothini, 2024; Gorksi & Swalwell, 2015).

or language proficiency and instead analyze the broader classroom structures that might contribute to this pattern. They might ask: *Are students being given enough time to process and share their thoughts? Are we valuing different ways of explaining math ideas, or are we privileging one dominant way of communicating?* In response, the teacher could implement strategies, such as allowing students to discuss in small groups before sharing with the class, using multiple representations (e.g., visual models, gestures, home languages), and validating diverse problem-solving approaches. By making these intentional shifts, the teacher is not just accommodating multilingual students but actively disrupting the inequitable structures that can silence them. This example highlights how the Equity Literacy Framework moves beyond a passive understanding of equity and instead positions teachers as critical agents of change in creating fair, just, and inclusive math classrooms.

Equity-Based Math Teaching Practices

In addition to the Equity Literacy Framework (Gorski & Pothini, 2024; Gorksi & Swalwell, 2015), equity-based math teaching practices can be explored. Aguirre et al. (2024) offer five equity-based practices that center on the idea that all students bring valuable knowledge, experiences, and ways of thinking that should be recognized and leveraged in the classroom (see Figure 2.1). These practices focus on positioning students as capable math thinkers, fostering meaningful math discourse, and using students' cultural and linguistic knowledge as assets

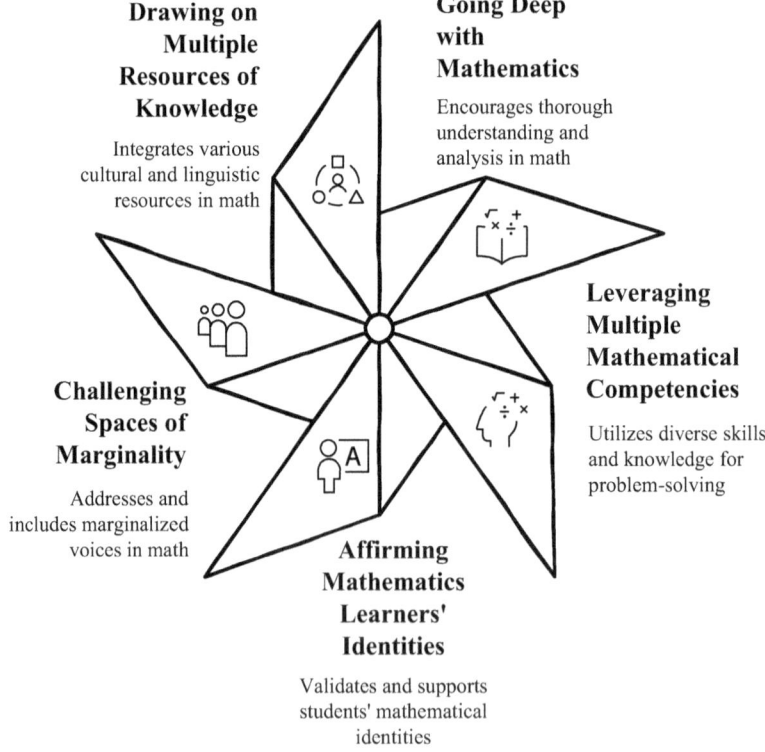

FIGURE 2.1 Equity-Based Math Teaching Practices.

Note: Adapted from Aguirre et al.'s (2024) Equity-Based Math Teaching Practices.

in learning. Instead of assuming that some students naturally excel in math while others struggle due to internal deficits, equity-based teaching requires teachers to create an environment where every student has opportunities to engage deeply, share their reasoning, and see their identities reflected in the learning process. This means intentionally designing lessons that invite multiple perspectives, encouraging collaboration, and using instructional strategies that affirm students' diverse math strengths. By shifting from a deficit mindset to an asset-based approach, teachers can help students develop positive math identities and a sense of belonging in the subject.

For example, imagine a third-grade teacher introducing a lesson on multiplication by exploring patterns in everyday life. Instead of presenting multiplication strictly through abstract equations, the teacher asks students to bring in or describe examples of multiplicative reasoning from their own experiences, such as doubling recipes at home, recognizing repeated patterns in cultural textiles, or organizing equal groups in family or community settings. As students share, the teacher values each contribution, drawing connections between their lived experiences and formal math concepts. This not only validates students' backgrounds but also enhances their conceptual understanding by making learning more relevant and meaningful. Additionally, during class discussions, the teacher encourages students to explain their reasoning in their own words, using their home languages if needed, before translating into mathematical notation. Thus, students' cultural and linguistic resources are seen as strengths rather than obstacles, fostering a classroom where all students feel empowered to engage with math (Aguirre et al., 2024; Bartell et al., 2017). However, achieving this student positioning requires intentional shifts in our pedagogical approach. It means moving away from deficit-oriented thinking, where we focus on what students "lack", and instead adopting an anti-deficit lens, where we recognize and build upon the strengths, knowledge, and experiences that students bring to the classroom.

Building on these equity-based math teaching practices (Aguirre et al., 2024), it is essential to consider how we, as teachers, notice and interpret students' math thinking and participation.

The way we perceive student engagement, reasoning, and problem-solving abilities shapes the instructional choices we make and the opportunities we provide. To deepen our commitment to equitable math teaching, we must critically examine our noticing practices, including what we attend to, how we interpret it, and how we respond. In the coming sections, we will explore how noticing frameworks can help us become more aware of our interpretations of students' math abilities and engagement. Specifically, we will introduce the FAIR Framework (Louie et al., 2021), which challenges deficit narratives and encourages a strengths-based perspective on student learning. Ultimately, our goal is not just to discuss equity but to develop intentional noticing skills that allow us to create math classrooms where every student feels seen, valued, and supported in their learning.

What Does It Mean to Notice? Introducing Noticing Frameworks

Noticing frameworks offer a powerful tool for teachers to become more intentional about what we pay attention to in the classroom, how we interpret what we see, and how we respond to our students. In math education, frameworks that focus on *attending*, *interpreting*, and *responding* have been widely used to help teachers recognize and analyze students' math thinking (Jacobs et al., 2010; Sherin et al., 2011). By using these frameworks, teachers can develop a sharper awareness of student strategies, identify patterns in their reasoning, and provide more targeted support.

However, noticing is not just about tracking individual thought processes, for it is also shaped by broader systems, expectations, and biases that influence what we see and how we make sense of it (Louie et al., 2021). Without realizing it, we may overlook the ways students engage with math in favor of more traditional markers of success, reinforcing narratives about who is "good at math." This is where equity-focused adaptations of noticing frameworks become essential.

If we are not careful, our noticing can fall into *deficit patterns*, where we unintentionally focus more on what students struggle with rather than recognizing their strengths (Adiredja & Louie, 2020). By shifting our noticing practices, we can disrupt these patterns and create a classroom culture that values the knowledge and abilities all students bring. This means expanding how we attend to student thinking, reinterpreting what success looks like, and responding in ways that empower rather than marginalize.

To make noticing more equitable, researchers have expanded these frameworks to better reflect the real-world dynamics of teaching. For example, Wager (2014) introduced the idea of positionality in noticing, which highlights how our own identities and experiences shape what we see in students. If you believe that sharing math ideas is cheating, then you might interpret students talking during math class as off-task or disruptive behavior. However, if you believe that people learn from one another's ideas, then you might interpret the same situation as students collaborating and problem-solving. Shah and Coles (2020) explored racialized noticing, pointing out that teachers, often without realizing it, may notice and interpret students' behaviors and abilities differently based on race. These adaptations remind us that noticing isn't just neutral, It's shaped by our perspectives, our teaching experiences, our training, and even larger cultural narratives about who does math. That's why Louie et al. (2021) created the FAIR Framework, which adds an important fourth component to attending, interpreting, and responding noted as *framing*. This shift helps us recognize that noticing is not just about student thinking, for it's also about the lenses we use to interpret what we see and the assumptions we bring with us.

A Framework for Challenging Deficit Thinking in Math Education

Louie et al.'s (2021) FAIR Framework can help us move away from deficit thinking and toward a more *anti-deficit* approach in our math classrooms. The FAIR Framework encourages us to (a) focus on students' assets and strengths, (b) attend to their math thinking rather than assumptions about ability, (c) identify and challenge deficit narratives, and (d) respond with equitable instructional choices. Instead of unconsciously reinforcing the idea that some students just "aren't math people," the FAIR Framework helps us reframe our perceptions and see the strengths each student brings. It also reminds us that what we notice, and how we interpret it—shapes the opportunities we provide for our students. By making our noticing more intentional and equity-focused, we can create learning environments where *all* students feel seen, valued, and capable of success in math.

Take, for example, a scenario of a student struggling to articulate their reasoning on a word problem. A traditional, deficit-based response might be to assume the student lacks understanding or the skills to engage in the math task. However, using the FAIR Framework, we shift our perspective and ask the following questions:

- What strategies is this student already using?
- How can this student reflect on their prior experiences and interests to make connections to the math content?
- How can I provide more opportunities for them to communicate their thinking in non-verbal ways?

Similarly, consider a group of students who speak a language other than English at home. Rather than viewing this as a barrier to learning math, the FAIR Framework encourages us to ask the following:

- How can this student's multilingual knowledge be an asset in math discussions?
- What visual or hands-on support could deepen their understanding?
- How can I position this student to use their multilingual knowledge to encourage peers to make connections between their languages and math concepts?

By focusing on what the student *does* understand, what experiences and strengths they bring to the problem, and what strategies might be used to scaffold their ability to express their thinking, we can create a pathway for growth instead of reinforcing a narrative of struggle and deficiencies.

Louie et al. (2021) emphasize that deficit discourses are often ingrained in educational practices, even when teachers have the best intentions. Deficit thinking can subtly emerge in how we describe students—labeling them as "low" or assuming that some students "just aren't math people." The FAIR Framework helps us actively challenge these narratives.

For instance, when a student approaches a problem differently than expected, a deficit-oriented response might be to redirect them to the "right way" of solving it. Instead, the FAIR Framework invites us to ask: *What math reasoning is embedded in their approach? How can I encourage them to refine and build on their ideas?* By shifting from correction to curiosity, we send a powerful message: *your thinking is valuable.*

The FAIR Framework doesn't just help us notice differently—it also challenges us to respond in ways that promote equity. This might mean rethinking how we group students, ensuring that all learners have access to high-level tasks, or making space for multiple ways of solving problems. For example, if we notice that certain students are consistently disengaged, rather than assuming they lack motivation, the FAIR Framework encourages us to consider: *Are the tasks culturally relevant and meaningful to them? Do they see themselves reflected in the math content?* When we design instruction with these questions in mind, we create a more inclusive and empowering learning environment. Thus, the FAIR Framework serves as a guide, one that we leverage in this book, for disrupting deficit thinking and helping us recognize the brilliance and potential in every student. By integrating an *asset-based lens* into our daily teaching, we move closer to a vision of math education that is truly equitable and just.

Moving Forward to Build a Culture of Anti-Deficit Noticing

Shifting our noticing practices to focus on students' strengths rather than their perceived deficits isn't something that happens

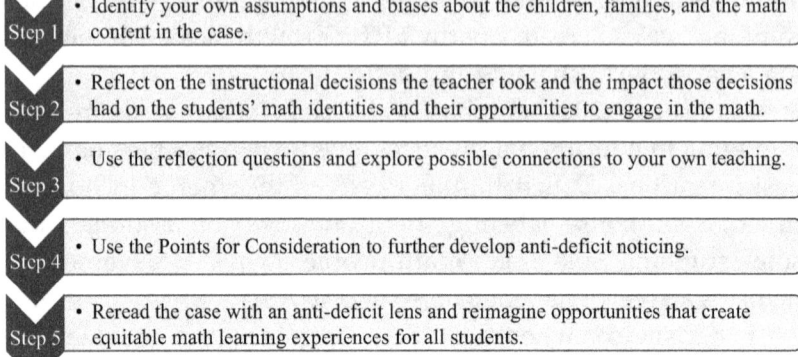

FIGURE 2.2 Process for Analyzing Cases Using Anti-Deficit Noticing.

overnight. It's an ongoing process of reflection, learning, and intentional action. The key is to start small by simply becoming more aware of what we're noticing in our classrooms. See Figure 2.2 for a suggested process to guide the analysis of cases using anti-deficit noticing.

Step 1

A great first step is to slow down and ask yourself: *What am I noticing? What assumptions might I be making?* We can use the following cases in this book to encourage mindful reflection about our assumptions and biases about children, their families, and the math content. Building reflection skills focused on targeted noticings and the impact such noticings have on instructional decisions and students can serve as a first step in the right direction. Step 1 should also be used in your own teaching. Taking a moment to pause and reflect, either in the middle of a lesson or at the end, can help us reframe how we see our students and their math thinking.

Step 2

After familiarizing yourself with a case, it is important to reflect on the teacher's instructional decisions and consider how those choices shape students' math identities and learning opportunities. By analyzing the rationale behind specific teaching strategies, such as the integration of community issues, the framing of math tasks, or the use of student-centered dialogue, we gain insight into how instruction can either affirm or marginalize students' experiences. This reflection helps illuminate whether students are positioned as capable problem-solvers and active participants in their learning or are simply passive recipients of information. It also encourages us to critically examine how our own practices promote equity, access, and agency in the classroom. Engaging in this type of reflection supports the development of more intentional, equity-oriented teaching that fosters meaningful math engagement for all students.

Step 3

Another strategy to support anti-deficit noticing is the use of intentional reflection questions and making connections to your own teaching practice. As you read through the cases in the following chapters, we encourage you to pause and reflect on the instructional moves made by the teacher and how they shaped students' engagement and identities in math. Use the reflection questions to guide your thinking and explore how the FAIR Framework (Louie et al., 2021) might prompt different interpretations or responses in your own classroom. Consider how the teacher's noticing compares to your own and what opportunities exist to shift your perspective toward more equitable, student-centered noticing. These reflections not only deepen personal insight but also lay the groundwork for meaningful changes in practice that affirm students' brilliance and lived experiences.

Step 4

To develop anti-deficit noticing, we can use other "points for consideration" as a springboard for collaborative dialogue. These points are designed to provoke deeper thinking about teacher noticing and provide entry points for examining how instructional decisions shape students' opportunities and identities in math. When we reflect on these prompts with colleagues, whether through co-analyzing student work, discussing case studies, or watching lesson recordings, we not only refine our individual perspectives but also cultivate a shared commitment to more equitable noticing. Engaging in this kind of collaborative inquiry, grounded in the FAIR Framework (Louie et al., 2021), supports a collective shift away from deficit-based interpretations toward recognizing students' strengths and brilliance. As you work through the cases, we encourage you to discuss the points for consideration in a professional learning community or with a trusted colleague, using them to surface new insights, challenge assumptions, and co-develop strategies that foster more just and inclusive math classrooms.

Just as we ask students to build understanding through dialogue, we benefit from doing the same as professionals. Engaging in a think-pair-share routine with colleagues—beginning with individual reflection on a case, followed by paired discussion, and culminating in a broader group conversation—creates space to examine our interpretations and surface the implicit beliefs that shape our noticing. These structured interactions invite us to question what we attend to, how we interpret student thinking, and how our perspectives are expanded or challenged through dialogue. When grounded in a shared framework like that of the FAIR Framework (Louie et al., 2021), these conversations can lead to concrete shifts in how we design instruction and position students as capable math thinkers. Ultimately, working through cases in community allows us to turn reflection into action, supporting a collective movement toward more humanizing and equity-centered math teaching.

Step 5

Finally, returning to the case with an anti-deficit lens invites us to reimagine what is possible for each student and uncover new ways to foster equitable math learning. By rereading with fresh eyes, we can identify moments where students' strengths may have been overlooked or underutilized and consider alternative instructional moves that could better affirm their math identities. This process encourages us to shift from simply noticing what happened to envisioning what *could* happen with intentional, equity-focused choices. As we engage in this step, we also open up space to ask: *How might I adapt my own practice to highlight student assets more clearly? What opportunities can I design to ensure every learner feels seen, supported, and challenged?* Revisiting cases in this way helps sustain our growth as reflective practitioners and deepens our commitment to cultivating justice-oriented classrooms where all students can thrive.

When reading the cases that follow, we encourage you to reflect on how you might respond in similar situations. Consider asking yourself: *What did the teacher notice? What might they have missed? How would I have responded in this moment, and why?* You may wish to record your responses to the reflection questions, drawing connections to your personal experiences and your classroom. You may also use the cases and the associated points for consideration to extend your thinking about particular topics. However you use the cases, know that reflecting on noticing patterns toward a more asset-based approach will deepen our ability to build relationships, honor the diverse ways students engage with math, and create an environment where every learner feels seen and valued. Case-based reflection doesn't just help us become better teachers—it helps us become more reflective, responsive, and inclusive teachers who recognize and celebrate the brilliance in all students.

3

Cases About Math Classroom Community Norms, Policies, and Procedures

As math teachers, we work hard to create a learning environment where all students feel safe, supported, and ready to engage with math concepts. To do this, we establish community norms, classroom policies, and procedures that help guide student behavior, promote collaboration, and ensure that our lessons run smoothly. These considerations are some of the things we have direct control over, such as how we structure group work, encourage student participation, and handle mistakes as part of the learning process.

However, there are also policies and procedures that extend beyond our classrooms, such as the rules set at the school, district, or even state level. These rules might include how students are placed in math groups, the curriculum pacing guides or scripts we are required to follow, standardized testing requirements, or school-wide behavior policies. While these policies are often designed with good intentions, they can sometimes have unintended consequences that impact equity in our classrooms.

The cases in this chapter take a closer look at both types of policies—those we create as teachers and those that come from outside our classrooms. Each case provides a brief description of the policies or procedures in place, but the real focus is on how teachers respond to the policies and procedures and the influence of such actions that impact equity in the elementary math classroom. As you read the following cases, consider how certain policies unintentionally create barriers for some students. Given the policies and procedures, do they reinforce existing disparities, or do they help bridge gaps in learning opportunities? How might you respond if you experienced similar situations?

By examining these cases, we can reflect on our own classroom practices and consider how we can advocate for changes, both small and large, that make math learning more accessible and meaningful for all students. After all, we know that every child brings unique strengths and needs to the classroom, and it's our job to create an environment where all students see themselves as capable and confident mathematicians. Additional points for consideration for these cases can be found in Chapter 7.

The following equity cases are included:

- *Case 3.1 First-Year Classroom Management* – Ms. Floyd, a first-year kindergarten teacher, struggles with classroom management despite implementing strict classroom procedures. During a math lesson, her rigid teaching style leaves a student confused and afraid to ask questions, reinforcing negative feelings toward math. This case highlights the importance of balancing structure with student interaction to foster a supportive and equitable learning environment.
- *Case 3.2 Differing Perspectives on Teaching Math Word Problems* – Leticia Agular, a previous fourth-grade math teacher, faces resistance from her new third-grade team when she proposes integrating reading comprehension strategies into math instruction to improve students' performance on word problems. The case highlights equity concerns, particularly the impact of deficit thinking about multilingual learners' reading abilities during math instruction. Leticia grapples with how to advocate for more effective strategies while adhering to school policies requiring instructional consistency across classrooms.

- *Case 3.3 Managing Manipulatives to Avoid Mishap* – Ms. Fisher, a second-year, second-grade teacher, struggles to manage math manipulatives equitably while maintaining classroom structure. Following a colleague's advice, she assigns specific students as Material Leaders, limiting access to the manipulatives. As she observes the impact of this policy, she questions whether it unintentionally excludes certain students, particularly those with disabilities, and reinforces implicit biases about who is "capable" of hands-on learning.
- *Case 3.4 One Teacher's Push for Inclusive Policies Beyond the Classroom* – Mr. Moss, a fourth-grade teacher, works to make out-of-school assignment policies more inclusive by considering his students' diverse backgrounds and access to resources. He navigates challenges, such as language barriers, limited family support, and rigid homework policies, by seeking guidance from colleagues, connecting families to community resources, and adjusting his approach to provide more flexibility. His efforts highlight the importance of questioning existing policies and making small yet meaningful changes to promote equity in student learning.
- *Case 3.5 Identifying Students for the Gifted Program* – Ms. Davis is a fifth-grade math teacher who notices a student whose high scores on tests and low scores on classwork do not align. Through creating a task that challenges her students to justify their solutions, the student becomes more engaged in classwork and demonstrates a deeper understanding of the order of operations. Ms. Davis then questions the student's prior teachers to learn why he was never tested for the gifted program.

Case 3.1 First-Year Classroom Management

Ms. Floyd just started her first job teaching kindergarten at a low-income, racially diverse elementary school. She is the only first-year teacher out of the six teachers in her kindergarten grade-level team, and her team gave her advice on how to manage her new group of 5-year-olds. The other kindergarten teachers shared classroom management techniques like procedures for students getting their own materials and for gaining students' attention using rhymes and chants. They also shared their lesson plans so that every kindergarten section keeps the same pacing and teaches the lessons in the same way. Still, Ms. Floyd feels confident that she knows how to manage a group of young children since she has helped raise many children in her family. She told her grade-level team, "Young kids need structure. I don't need to use all those cutesy ideas. I can't be soft, or they will run all over me." Ms. Floyd will ensure her students stay on track with the lessons her grade level uses by enforcing strict expectations. She created detailed schedules and procedures for her students to follow so that they would know exactly what to do every minute of the school day, including having students keep a bubble in their mouths and hands to themselves. Ms. Floyd was sure this would prevent misbehavior since all the students would be busy with their studies.

Once school started, Ms. Floyd often lost her temper with her students. No matter how many times she reminded her students about the rules and procedures, her students would frequently forget or choose to talk with one another. One example was during a math lesson on how to make ten. Ms. Floyd called all the students to their assigned seats on the carpet to show them how to make ten so they could complete the worksheet that the kindergarten teachers decided to use with their students. The worksheet had ten equations written on the paper: ___ + ___ = 10. Ms. Floyd said, "Today, you will learn what numbers make ten when added together. I will show you an easy way to complete this work, but first, raise your hand if you can count to ten."

The students in the class silently raised their hands. Ms. Floyd looked around the room and responded, "Good. Then, you will be able to finish this worksheet easily. Do you see these blank spaces?" Ms. Floyd pointed to the first blanks in each equation for the first addend, and the students nodded. Ms. Floyd said, "You will start at 0 and write each number 0 through 9 down this spot. Then, you will start at the bottom and write 0 through 9, moving up along this second spot." Ms. Floyd moved her finger up the column of blank spots meant for the second addend in each equation.

She asked, "Charles, what are you supposed to do?" Charles looked startled and replied, "Write the numbers." Ms. Floyd rolled her eyes and raised her voice to say, "What numbers? Where are you supposed to write it? I need you all to listen to me."

Charles's eyes began to water as Ms. Floyd continued, "Everyone, repeat after me. Write the numbers 0 through 9 down this spot." The students repeated. "Good. Now write 0 through 9 moving up this spot." The students repeated the last step. Ms. Floyd felt better about the students knowing how to complete the math worksheet, so she sent the students back to their seats to work independently.

Once the students got back to their seats, Charles was upset. He felt embarrassed for being called out in front of the class and was confused about what to do on the paper. He knew he needed to write the numbers, but the teacher said to start with a number other than 1. He did not remember which number to begin with, and he was worried because he forgot how to write the number 2.

Charles leans over to look at Malik's paper and asks, "What did you write?" Malik whispers, "0." Charles was about to ask another question when Ms. Floyd yelled, "Charles, you know you are not supposed to be talking right now. It looks like you have lost your recess time. Next time, you will remember not to talk." Charles could not hold it in any longer and began to cry. Ms. Floyd sighed and said, "Get a tissue and get back to work." As the students were working and Charles was still sniffling, Ms. Floyd began questioning her interaction with Charles and if she may have reacted too harshly.

Reflection Questions

1. What kind of classroom environment has Ms. Floyd created? How might this lesson or the classroom environment impact how Charles sees himself as a math learner? How might other students have been impacted by watching the interaction between Charles and Ms. Floyd?
2. How did Ms. Floyd's instructions on the math worksheet impact students' understanding of how to make ten? What would you have done to help students understand this math concept?
3. Ms. Floyd believed that her students should keep a bubble in their mouths and independently focus on their studies. How could Ms. Floyd leverage students' desire to collaborate and engage in conversations into her math instruction?
4. What rules and procedures have you implemented in your classroom that build a positive classroom environment where students can develop their math identities?

Case 3.2 Differing Perspectives on Teaching Math Word Problems

Leticia Agular had been a fourth-grade math teacher for the past five years. She served as the fourth-grade math lead teacher and worked with the other grade-level math teachers to improve student performance on the state math exams by helping students make sense of word problems. The principal was impressed with Leticia's efforts in fourth grade, so Leticia was moved to the third-grade team to improve those math scores, since they have maintained a 60% pass rate.

The third-grade team is self-contained, which means the teachers are responsible for teaching all core subjects to the same group of students. The school's policy requires consistency across the third-grade sections regarding lesson planning, assignments, and assessments. Leticia knows some of the teachers on the third-grade team have a reputation for being difficult to work with, and maintaining consistency across their sections will be a challenge. However, she is excited to teach third grade because she knows she can incorporate word problem comprehension into her reading lessons as a self-contained teacher.

There are six teachers on the third-grade team. Ken and Mandy are first-year teachers. Priya taught fourth-grade reading for 2 years, and this is her second year teaching third-grade. Carol has taught third grade for the past 5 years at the school and has been the lead teacher for the third-grade team. Allison taught various grade levels at the school for 17 years, but she has primarily been a third-grade teacher. These teachers and Leticia met to discuss the upcoming school year to discuss their semester plans and prepare for the first week of school.

Allison started the meeting off by saying, "Ok! The faster we get this done, the faster we can begin working in our classrooms. We have the plans from last year. Carol, would you mind sharing it with Ken, Mandy, and Leticia?"

Carol nodded and began to look at her computer for the plans from the previous school year.

Leticia said, "Thank you for sharing those plans. I look forward to reading through them as we plan this year. I want to talk about the state math test and what the team has done to prepare for it in the past."

Allison rolled her eyes and said, "These kids are below grade level and still can't read like they need to, especially all the ELLs. You are much better off focusing on the reading test because if they can't read, they can't do math. I will give you a copy of the CUBES poster we use to prepare them for the math test. That strategy works fine for math because the low readers only need to learn a few words to get through the test."

Mandy asked, "What is the CUBES strategy?" Allison replied, "It's an acronym to help with word problems. Circle the numbers, underline the question, box the keywords, eliminate extra information, and solve the problem. I will send everyone a copy. Are we done here?"

Priya said, "We still need to pick a lead teacher."

Allison immediately said, "Not it!"

Carol said, "I don't mind doing it again if no one else wants it."

Ken and Mandy looked around the room to wait for what the others had to say. Allison and Priya shrugged their shoulders in agreement.

Leticia felt frustrated that no one seemed willing to talk about the plans for the upcoming school year like they were supposed to be doing. Leticia said, "I am OK with Carol being the lead, but we have not discussed our plans for this year. Having taught fourth grade, I know that the students go to fourth grade needing additional help with reading comprehension, particularly with math problems. I can share what we have done to improve word problem comprehension with fourth grade so that we can all start using it this year. The consistency across the grade levels will help our students progress from grade to grade."

Allison looked frustrated and said, "I know what works with these kids and what doesn't. The CUBES strategy works, even with those ELLs. We are not changing what we are doing. I am going to work in my classroom now." She got up and left.

Carol looked apologetically at the rest of the team and dismissed herself to go to her classroom. Ken and Mandy looked uneasy and a bit overwhelmed, but they also left to go to their classrooms.

Priya stayed behind and told Leticia, "She is like this all the time, and she won't change her mind. I know what you did in fourth grade worked well, but many of these kids are behind grade-level reading. The CUBES strategy helps them identify keywords and numbers that can help them solve some math problems even if they have trouble with reading comprehension."

Leticia felt defeated and replied, "It just feels like we are giving up on helping these kids improve their reading and math problem-solving since the CUBES strategy is not focused on reading comprehension. What will the students do when the word problems don't have keywords? They need strategies to make sense of these word problems and then practice those strategies. I have ideas that can help all kids, including our ELLs, understand math word problems, but no one was willing to listen."

Priya said, "I know. I will discuss it with you after we set up our classrooms, but we need a majority vote to change anything our team does. You won't get Allison on your side, and the new teachers will go with whatever is easiest right now. Let everyone get set up for the school year, and then we can try talking about it again."

Leticia left the room feeling frustrated and defeated. She knows the school policy requires consistency with lesson plans across all third-grade sections. She thinks to herself, "The CUBES strategy does more harm than good. I can't teach it. Should I just do what I know worked with my fourth-graders? I know all my students, including ELLs, can solve math word problems."

Reflection Questions
1 Why is Leticia pushing back on the CUBES strategy?
2 How does Allison's view of what students need to know to do math limit her students' learning opportunities?
3 How can a teacher's deficit view of children's reading ability, particularly multilingual children's reading ability, impact math instruction?

4 Given the school's requirement for consistency, how might Leticia introduce new strategies while maintaining alignment with her team? What role does school leadership (e.g., principal, instructional coaches) play in influencing math instruction? How could they support Leticia in advocating for change?
5 How have you worked with a team that disagreed with math instructional strategies and practices? What did you do to advocate for your insights?
6 What are strategies for helping all students, particularly multilingual students, with comprehending and solving word problems?

Case 3.3 Managing Manipulatives to Avoid Mishap

During back-to-school planning, Ms. Fisher reflected on her first year of teaching and how challenging it was to manage students' use of math manipulatives. It is only her second year of teaching second-grade in a self-contained classroom, so she decided to reach out to Ms. Howell, the first-grade teacher, for advice.

Ms. Howell told her, "Be ready for this group of students coming your way! I hope they matured over the summer because they were careless with manipulatives last year. Some kids, like Melvin, liked to throw and break anything they could get their hands on. For other kids like Amina, it is more hassle than it's worth to help her use the manipulatives. You may want to assign Material Leaders and limit who works with your manipulatives. Take it from me, you won't regret it!"

Ms. Fisher knows the importance of using manipulatives to make sense of place value and regrouping strategies when adding and subtracting. In a recent conversation with her math instructional coach, Ms. Baker shared, "Try using base ten blocks when teaching place value and regrouping strategies with your students instead of other manipulatives like Unifix or snap cubes."

With this in mind, Ms. Fisher added base ten blocks to her nicely organized manipulatives bookshelf at the back of her classroom. She then made a sign above the manipulative bookshelf detailing her procedures for student use of manipulatives. The sign notes four rules:

- ♦ Rule #1 – One math manipulative tub per group when approved.
- ♦ Rule #2 – Material Leaders must retrieve and return the manipulative tub to the bookshelf when instructed to do so.
- ♦ Rule #3 – Math manipulatives must stay on the Material Leaders' desks and are only to be used by the Material Leaders.
- ♦ Rule #4 – Material Leaders must be responsible with the manipulatives and use them as directed.

Ms. Fisher hoped that the rules would help her have a successful year with her students when working with math manipulatives.

After one month of school, Ms. Fisher was ready to teach the regrouping strategies using place value to her students. In planning for the lessons, Ms. Fisher reflected on her students' needs, including those with individualized education programs (IEPs) and her one student, Amina, with a 504 plan, who has a physical disability that affects her fine motor skills. Ms. Fisher thought to herself, "I want to create small groups of four students that can explore the base ten blocks that Ms. Baker suggested. To help maintain classroom safety and structure, I'll be strategic when assigning groups and the Material Leaders."

One of her students, Melvin, has an IEP that specifies access to visuals and manipulatives to support his understanding of math concepts. When using materials, the IEP details how Ms. Fisher must provide materials and closely monitor their use. Yet, Melvin also struggles with impulse control, and Ms. Fisher has observed him throwing crayons and erasers when he gets frustrated. She often yells at Melvin, "Sit on your hands and watch the leader." Ms. Fisher thought to herself, "I'll assign Melvin to groups where a Material Leader will properly use the manipulatives to address Melvin's IEP and ensure the rules are followed."

Being mindful of the 504 plan, Ms. Fisher does the same for Amina. Ms. Fisher thought to herself, "The blocks could help Amina understand the algorithm better, but I know she has trouble moving the blocks around without assistance. I should probably ask around about what other manipulatives could be helpful for Amina, but I don't want it to seem like I am questioning the base ten blocks that Ms. Baker suggested."

Ms. Fisher's solution was to make sure Amina was not assigned as the Material Leader.

As the students continued to work in groups through the place value unit, Ms. Fisher began wondering how her implicit biases might affect her decisions when grouping students and assigning roles. She noticed herself feeling more hesitant to give materials to certain students, like Amina and Melvin, and she wonders if she is unfairly assuming they "can't handle it."

She also noticed that both Melvin and Amina were disappointed that they had never been assigned the Material Leader. Amina was overheard saying to her group members, "You all got to be the Material Leader. I know it might take me longer to count out the little blocks to make trades, but I think I can do it to regroup and subtract 27 from 61."

One of her group members said, "We can't break Rule #3 because then we would lose recess time. The blocks have to stay on my desk."

Ms. Fisher began to question who she gives access to the base ten blocks and if limiting the role of the Material Leader is helping or hurting students' learning opportunities. She asks herself,

> "How might students feel if only a few classmates have access to the manipulatives while the rest are expected to learn without them? I don't want to be unfair. I know, I'll model the manipulatives myself. This will save time and the worry about tending to students' individualized needs."

As the unit continues, Ms. Fisher is the one modeling manipulatives in front of her classroom. While some students made comments about wanting to get hands-on with the manipulatives, she knows no one is being singled out when not assigned the Material Leader. However, she begins to question her new strategy and asks herself, "Am I doing the right thing to maintain an inclusive environment? Maybe I should just forget to use math manipulatives altogether! What should I do?"

Reflection Questions

1 Why might Ms. Baker encourage Ms. Fisher to use base ten blocks when teaching place value and regrouping strategies with her students instead of other manipulatives like Unifix or snap cubes?
2 How might Ms. Fisher's perceptions of her students, influenced by the feedback received from last year's teacher, impact her decisions about providing access to manipulatives? Are there ways she could reframe these perceptions to ensure all students are given a fair chance?

3 In what ways might implicit biases around behavior and ability influence Ms. Fisher's thoughts about who "can handle" manipulatives? How can she become more aware of these biases to promote equity in her classroom?
4 How can Ms. Fisher balance classroom management concerns with the goal of equitable access to manipulatives? What strategies might help her support students who need manipulatives without removing their access due to behavioral concerns?
5 How could Ms. Fisher better tailor her approach to meet individual needs, such as those of students with IEPs or physical disabilities, without unintentionally creating barriers or singling students out?
6 How might Ms. Fisher get feedback from her students about their math experiences in an ongoing and authentic manner? How does asking for this feedback from her students shift power in the classroom setting?
7 What role do teachers' assumptions and experiences play in decisions about equity and access in the classroom? How might you reflect on your assumptions to promote a more inclusive learning environment?

Case 3.4 One Teacher's Push for Inclusive Policies Beyond the Classroom

In a diverse fourth-grade math classroom, Mr. Moss wants to create out-of-school assignment policies reflecting students' unique backgrounds and needs. He knows that some students come from varied cultural, linguistic, and socioeconomic backgrounds, which can impact how they complete homework and projects at home. To guide Mr. Moss in planning his upcoming unit on division, Mr. Moss wonders, "How can I implement assignments that consider the complexity of my students' language barriers, family engagement, and disparities in access to resources?"

Mr. Moss knows he has many students whose families want to support their learning but face language barriers. While his school has a sizable population of bilingual students, the resources for translating assignment instructions are limited. Mr. Moss initially tried to use online translation tools, but they often produced confusing or incorrect translations that frustrated families. He recalls his student Rico, who shared, "My mamá tried to help me complete the fraction equivalence compare and contrast worksheet but couldn't read the written examples. I tried drawing a picture about the problem to make sense of it, but it was too hard for us to figure out what we needed to do."

Mr. Moss wants to ensure that his assignments are clear and accessible, and he does not want family members to struggle through inadequate translations or feel unable to support their children's education. He wonders, "Who can I contact at school to learn about resources available to my students and their families?"

Mr. Moss also notices that while some of his students have supportive environments at home—quiet spaces, adult help, and access to learning materials—others lack support due to various economic and social factors. He is concerned about how homework and project policies might unintentionally penalize students without the means to complete assignments to the same standards as their peers. For example, while some students share how they go to after-school tutoring and enrichment programs, others cannot attend.

The other day, Camila told Mr. Moss, "Daniela offered to take me to the library across town to get help on the project, but I had to help my big sister watch our little brother because my mom had to work a second shift. I couldn't get help from the library to complete my assignment due today. Can I have another day to try going to the library again?"

Mr. Moss follows classroom expectations and out-of-school assignment policies that closely align with the school's policies on assigning and grading homework. The school expects fourth-grade teachers to assign 15–20 minutes of math homework at least three times a week. Three weekly trips to a library may not be possible to receive support. Additionally, families may be unable to provide one-on-one support with working through a math workbook every other night.

Mr. Moss feels torn between following these established policies and advocating for his students. Recognizing that policies and grading at the school come from a one-size-fits-all perspective, not accounting for the nuances of his students' lives, Mr. Moss begins to consider ways to support his students without putting additional burdens on families. He starts by contacting the school's bilingual family liaison, Ms. Garcia, for advice on community resources.

Ms. Garcia informs him, "Some local community centers and libraries offer free tutoring sessions and study spaces for students. Some students find this helpful. And, the library in town has a bilingual staff member who is always willing to assist students and families with assignments."

Mr. Moss also discovers that he can access translation support through a district-provided language service, which could be valuable for keeping families informed and engaged.

For the next unit, Mr. Moss adjusts his homework policy to reflect a weekly homework packet due at the end of the week, allowing for more flexible out-of-school work options to take advantage of available support resources. He also offers feedback-based grades instead of penalizing students for late submissions. Furthermore, he sets up a classroom resource center where students can borrow donated supplies to complete assignments, like construction paper, markers, glue, and poster boards.

He thinks to himself, "I want to see if these small changes, within my control, work for my students. I plan to document my observations on how existing policies impact my class, such as specific examples of students who struggle with the current homework requirements due to external factors. Then, I want to see how my modified out-of-school assignment policy engages students differently. I can take my data to the administrators and see if it's possible to adjust school-wide policy recommendations to create more equitable learning environments for students."

Mr. Moss also schedules a meeting with the school's instructional support team, hoping they can provide guidance or help him advocate for policy adjustments. By engaging in these discussions, he notes, "I feel like a better advocate for my students, empowering them with assignment policies that are responsive to their realities. Advocating for my students doesn't always require a major policy overhaul. I can start with small changes that align with my students' needs and respect their home lives."

Reflection Questions

1. Mr. Moss tries to understand his students' individual needs and the limitations of existing out-of-school assignment policies. What are some considerations he reflects on, and why might these considerations be appropriate to support his students better?
2. Mr. Moss mentions how he contacted colleagues and the school's bilingual family liaison for advice on community resources. What were some resources he learned through this experience? Who might you contact at your school to learn about similar resources?
3. Mr. Moss sets up a space in his classroom where students can donate and borrow supplies for assignments. What are some things that you do in your classroom or that your school offers to support students with access to materials?
4. Families from different countries might solve math problems in different ways. How could Mr. Moss communicate math strategies taught in class with families that do not require those families to find translation services?

5. Mr. Moss may not have full authority to change schoolwide policies, but his willingness to challenge and adapt these norms in his classroom sets a meaningful example and fosters an inclusive and equitable learning environment. Reflect on your school's out-of-school assignment policies and other policies of interest. Are there any policies that make you question whether the expectations truly serve each of your students' learning journeys or, instead, reinforce existing inequities?

Case 3.5 Identifying Students for the Gifted Program

Ms. Davis is a fifth-grade math teacher who has recently completed a gifted certification program. One of the courses she completed had her look at her students' data on test scores and classwork to evaluate if those scores accurately represented her students' math understanding. Out of all her students, there was one student, Jamari, whom she felt she needed to closely examine.

Jamari is a Black boy who would receive high scores on tests but would have low grades on his class assignments. During class, he would talk with his peers or draw pictures, and when he turned in his work, it would often not be fully completed. Jamari's fourth-grade teacher called him a troublemaker, but Ms. Davis didn't think Jamari was a bad kid. In fact, she closely observed him during class and noticed that he would start on an assignment and get about halfway through before he would stop working and begin talking with his peers. After witnessing this behavior multiple times during one week, Ms. Davis decided to try something new with her math assignments. She typically would assign work from the curriculum that would have students practice a skill multiple times, but she wanted to challenge Jamari and the other students to think deeper about the math.

During the next class, Ms. Davis decided to create a new activity for the students to practice the order of operations that did not involve solving multiple problems. She launched the task by saying, "I saw a debate online that I want you to help me solve. When given the problem $6 \div 2(1 + 2)$, there are two answers everyone comes up with. They think the answer is either 9 or 1. Your job today is to figure out how they got each answer and develop an argument for which one is the correct answer. You can work with your small groups on this task so you can present your argument to the class."

Jamari's eyes lit up when he heard this task! He immediately got to work figuring out how there could be two different answers to the problem, and he shared both of those ideas with his group before they were done with their calculations. Jamari was the most engaged he had been in math class, and he took the lead in developing his group's argument for why they all agreed that the answer was 1.

During the groups' presentations, Jamari led his group's discussion, answered his peers' questions, and justified his thinking in more sophisticated ways than his classmates. Ms. Davis started to wonder if Jamari had been bored in math class, and that is why he often became off task to the point of not finishing his work. Maybe he wasn't challenged like he needed to be.

Ms. Davis knew that her school started testing for the gifted program in second grade. The procedure her school used for testing was that either a parent or a teacher had to recommend a student to be tested. Not very many parents were aware of this procedure, so usually testing for the gifted program was recommended by a student's teachers. Ms. Davis knew that Jamari was not in the gifted program, so she began looking into his records to see if he had ever been tested. Not seeing any notes, she went to Jamari's second-grade teacher and asked, "Did you ever recommend Jamari to be tested for the gifted program?"

The second-grade teacher looked confused and said, "Absolutely not. I didn't think his math was that impressive. He didn't complete tasks quickly, nor did he show his work. Why would I think he's gifted?" Ms. Davis thought that this narrative about Jamari was similar to what his fourth-grade teacher had said. She decided to ask his third-grade teacher if he had ever recommended Jamari for gifted testing. The third-grade teacher replied, "I don't typically recommend students for that test, and Jamari didn't make good grades in my class. He also seemed distracted, so I didn't think he could handle more challenging work."

Ms. Davis realized that Jamari had never been evaluated for the gifted program and suspected that his boredom in class might stem from a lack of academic challenge, especially in math. Although she knew it was uncommon to refer a student for gifted testing as late as fifth grade, she decided to recommend him anyway. At the same time, she began questioning the school's policy, which placed the responsibility on potentially uninformed parents and teachers whose judgments could be biased in their assumptions, instead of just testing all the students. She decided to raise this concern with the principal, believing it was an issue worth addressing to ensure students don't get overlooked for support and fall through the cracks.

Reflection Questions

1 Jamari has been labeled by teachers as "distracted" and a "troublemaker." Why are the labels particularly harmful to Jamari as a Black boy? How have these labels impacted his math identity?

2 What might have motivated Ms. Davis to modify the task? How did her decision impact student engagement and learning?

3 How does the new task about order of operations present students with a math challenge for the class? How might this task support students' problem-solving skills, reasoning, or math discourse compared to the previous tasks they've encountered?

4 Although Jamari's earlier math lessons are not detailed, what can you infer about the nature of the tasks his teachers may have used and the teachers' expectations for engaging in math? How might the structure and level of cognitive demand in those tasks have contributed to Jamari's current level of disengagement in math?

5 What is the current testing policy for the gifted program at your school? What revisions to this policy or related practices could help ensure that all students, including those who are often overlooked, have equitable opportunities to demonstrate their math potential through access to more rigorous and engaging math learning experiences?

4

Cases About Communication in Math Classrooms

When thinking about communication in math classrooms, you might have immediately thought about math discourse—students talking about their math thinking. While verbal exchanges are essential for promoting language development, active listening, and social interaction, they also serve a critical instructional purpose by providing teachers with real-time insight into students' understanding, allowing for more responsive and targeted teaching. However, effective math communication extends beyond spoken words. Students also convey their thinking through a range of representations, such as using manipulatives, creating drawings or diagrams, and using formal math notation. These varied modes of communication are equally valuable, as they offer multiple entry points for students to express their reasoning and make their thinking visible.

Children have a diverse array of needs when communicating in math class, and it is our goal to be inclusive so students can learn the math content to the best of their abilities. Some children might be multilingual and need to process the math content in their home language before translating to English. This extra processing for multilingual students requires much more thinking, so teachers may have these students communicate their math thinking in their home language or provide additional time to process. There might also be some students who are nonverbal and need to communicate their math thinking through different modalities like manipulatives, pictures, or communication devices. Ultimately, teachers play a central role in shaping the communicative culture of their classrooms by determining not only how often students are encouraged to share their thinking but also the forms that communication can take. Supporting diverse learners in developing a deeper and more flexible understanding of math will require teachers to examine the communication expectations for their classrooms.

The cases in this chapter center on the importance of communication and sharing a diversity of ideas when learning math. These cases demonstrate the power teachers hold when deciding whose ideas are heard and considered during math lessons. The teachers make decisions about who is called on to share solutions and strategies with the whole class, how students are expected to share their thinking, and what is considered a *correct* way to do math. All of these instructional decisions then communicate a message to students about who is valued during math lessons, which ultimately impacts students' math identities.

After examining these cases, reflect on the opportunities you provide for your students to communicate their math thinking. What does this communication look like? Whose ideas are regularly shared, and whose ideas need to be highlighted more often? What messages do your instructional decisions communicate to your students? Look for creative ways to encourage students to be a part of the math conversation in whatever way is best for them.

The following equity cases are included:

- *Case 4.1 Verbal and Nonverbal Communication* – Ms. Patel, a kindergarten teacher, calls on a select few students to share their ideas during whole-group discussions. A discussion between her and the paraprofessional prompts Ms. Patel to reflect on how she can provide opportunities for more students to communicate their thinking.
- *Case 4.2 Problems with Small Groups* – Ms. Morales, a second-year fifth-grade math teacher, has a conversation with a parent regarding a student's participation with

classmates during small group discussions. She considers implications for nonparticipation in group discussions on the students' math learning.
- *Case 4.3 Reframing and Valuing Student Voice* – Ms. Cho, a first-grade teacher, leads a class discussion about how to decompose an addend to benchmark ten as a strategy for addition. Students' strategies are discussed using informal and formal math vocabulary.
- *Case 4.4 Math Is a Universal Language?* – Mr. Ronduen, a new fourth-grade math teacher, mixes up student groups so that English is the only language of communication. Tension arises between him and a new student with place value notations used in different countries.
- *Case 4.5 Building Math Confidence Through Asset-Based Language* – Mr. Guyton, a kindergarten teacher, creates a classroom norm where students are positioned as capable mathematicians. His attention to using asset-based language is observed by a school administrator who asks him if he can lead a professional learning session to model for others ways he fosters math spaces where all students feel welcomed to share their math ideas.

Case 4.1 Verbal and Nonverbal Communication

Ms. Patel is a kindergarten teacher. Over the last few days, she has worked with her students to introduce them to the attributes of two-dimensional shapes. By now, most students are able to identify attributes of shapes, such as their size, color, and number of sides and vertices. To launch today's lesson, Ms. Patel shows a picture of a blue hexagon and asks students to open their math journals and write the shape's attributes. Students use the anchor charts in the room to help them write the attributes they notice.

As she walks around the classroom, she observes how Oliver, Kai, and Nova are quick to write in their journals. Ms. Patel asks Oliver to share the attributes he wrote down. In the second problem, Ms. Patel asks her students to draw a square and write its attributes. Again, Oliver, Kai, and Nova are quick to put their crayons down after drawing and writing in their math journals. Ms. Patel asks Kai to describe the square he drew.

With the students warmed up, thinking about the attributes of shapes, Ms. Patel asks the students to close their math journals and look up at the board. She says, "We are going to play a game called 'Guess My Sort.' I will show you three shapes that are all alike in some way. I need you to tell me the attribute that they have that is the same."

To begin, Ms. Patel shows a picture of the following:

1. A small, yellow rhombus
2. A small, blue trapezoid
3. A large, yellow square

Oliver, Kai, and Nova are the first ones to raise their hands. Ms. Patel calls on Oliver to share his answer, and he says, "The number of sides."

Ms. Patel says, "Wonderful, Oliver. Kai, can you tell me how many sides each shape has?"

He responds with, "Four."

Ms. Patel says, "Wonderful! All of these shapes are called quadrilaterals because they have four sides. Quadrilaterals can look different, but they still need to have four sides."

For the next problem, Ms. Patel shows a picture of the following:

1. An orange right triangle
2. A blue isosceles triangle
3. A blue equilateral triangle

Nova is the first to raise her hand to share her answer. Ms. Patel knows Nova is a nonverbal student and doesn't want to single her out by asking her to describe the sorting attribute. Instead, she calls on Levi to share his answer.

Levi correctly answers, "They all have three sides."

Ms. Patel asks, "What are shapes called with three sides?"

Many students in the class yell out, "Triangle!"

Ms. Patel says, "Yes! Triangles can all look different, but they still need to have three sides."

As Ms. Patel continues the game, she realizes she has only enough time to do one more round before specials. Recalling Oliver's correct responses thus far, she calls on him to share his answer so that other students can check their answers.

The paraprofessional, Ms. Johnson, notices who Ms. Patel called on to share their answers. Ms. Johnson and Ms. Patel have teamed taught since they started working together and have built a trusted relationship when it comes to debriefing students' needs.

As the students transition to specials, Ms. Johnson pulls Ms. Patel aside. She says, "Ms. Patel, I noticed during the lesson that Nova raised her hand to share her answer. I've been working to build Nova's confidence to contribute even if it might need to be through another format. I was excited to see Nova wanting to share, but she was never called on. During clean-up time, Nova showed me her recorded responses. I could tell she wanted to share her responses with the class."

Ms. Patel asks Ms. Johnson how Nova might be able to share next time. Ms. Johnson replies, "Nova is great at drawing pictures, so maybe she can describe her response through her drawings. She also has her tablet to select images, words, and numbers to communicate her thoughts. She could hold up her tablet and point to show her thinking to the class."

Ms. Patel hadn't considered some of the strategies Ms. Johnson shared with her. Encouraged by these strategies, she begins to wonder, "Who else am I not giving a voice to contribute in my class?"

Reflection Questions
1. In the Guess My Sort game, Ms. Patel shows a group of shapes with many different attributes that students could attend to. Why might she choose to do this?
2. Ms. Patel chose to introduce students to the word quadrilateral to describe four-sided polygons since they identified quadrilaterals that all looked a little different. When do you choose to make connections to math content that is beyond the grade level you teach?
3. Ms. Patel appears to call on students who have the correct answer or can respond in a way she has envisioned. What are the implications of this action on student learning, including how students communicate their math thinking?
4. How does Ms. Johnson advocate for Nova? How does her conversation with Ms. Patel give voice to Nova? What other ways could Ms. Johnson have advocated for Nova? How might you have handled the situation?
5. Ms. Johnson suggests some explicit strategies for lesson adaptations that support Nova's learning needs. How might these suggestions support and uplift math learning for everyone?
6. What are some ways that you help students communicate their math thinking in your classroom? What are the instructional implications of these strategies? How do your students respond?

Case 4.2 Problems with Small Groups

Ms. Morales is a second-year fifth-grade math teacher in a diverse school with students from many different countries who practice different religions. She loves the school's diversity and thinks it is beneficial for students to interact with and build friendships with so many others who are different from their own families and backgrounds. To build these friendships and interactions, Ms. Morales incorporates assigned seats where students are organized into groups to encourage collaborative discussions during her math lessons. She purposefully creates heterogeneous groups so that students sit with peers who speak different home languages, and she distributes the students as evenly as possible, given their identified gender and differing math strengths. Ms. Morales also changes up the groups every three to four weeks so her students can work with many different peers in the class.

Ms. Morales feels like she has created a positive relationship with her students and their families at this school, and she is surprised when a student's mother contacts her for a meeting after school. The email from Fatima's mother read, "Dear Ms. Morales, could we please meet today after school to discuss Fatima's assigned seat in your class? I am concerned and would like to discuss moving her seat immediately."

Ms. Morales is confused by this email and thinks, "Is there a problem? Fatima hasn't come to me with any issues." She quickly responds to Fatima's mother by writing, "Dear Mrs. Bakir, I would be happy to meet with you after school today. Would 3:00 pm work for your schedule? If so, I can inform the front office that we have a parent-teacher meeting."

Mrs. Bakir arrived for the meeting and hugged Ms. Morales, as they have a close relationship in a neighborhood gardening group. Then Mrs. Bakir said, "You know Fatima is often shy and reserved in class, and I want to discuss Fatima's assigned seat. As you noticed, Fatima is now at the age when she has started wearing her hijab. This transition reflects a time in a girl's life when she needs to be around other girls, so I would appreciate it if you could move her to an all-girl group in your class."

Ms. Morales was caught off guard by this request and said, "I mix up the groups so that all students have a chance to work with everyone in the class. This grouping approach allows them to hear different perspectives when problem-solving and builds community in the classroom. I do not make all-girl groups or all-boy groups, and the groups change many times during the school year. Fatima hasn't told me about having an issue with her group members. What has she shared with you?"

Ms. Bakir replied, "We try to keep girls separated from boys as much as possible now that she is at this age. Plus, Fatima feels uncomfortable with the boys in the class who ask her about the hijab. She tells me she doesn't want to talk to those boys, which ends in her feeling like some boys don't want to include her in the group. I am worried it will impact her grade in math class."

The news about Fatima's discomfort and her peers' interest in her hijab is surprising to Ms. Morales, but then she starts to think back to the beginning of the school year. Fatima used to be more engaged with class discussions in her small groups and with the whole class. Now she does seem quieter and withdrawn from the last two small groups she was assigned to join.

Ms. Morales says, "I will talk to Fatima to learn more about what her classmates are asking her about the hijab. Since other students in the class do not wear a hijab, it is important that I talk with the whole class about how we communicate and respect one another. I want to make sure Fatima feels safe in my class so she can continue to learn math to her best ability. I do not mind moving some of the groups, but I cannot guarantee that she will be in an all-girl group."

Ms. Bakir nodded and asked, "Can you at least ensure that the person sitting directly next to her is a girl?"

Ms. Morales smiled and responded, "Absolutely. I will also keep a closer eye on the groups to see how they are communicating. All my students must feel safe sharing their ideas with one another, including Fatima. Thank you so much for bringing this to my attention. After I talk with the class, I will talk with Fatima privately to avoid unwanted attention on her."

Reflection Questions

1. How does Ms. Morales use group work in her math class? What are her goals for using group work in these ways?
2. With deeper reflection, Ms. Morales realizes that Fatima's participation in class has shifted over the school year to become more withdrawn as she was assigned to new small groups. How could withdrawing from small group discussions impact Fatima's math learning?
3. How might a teacher with a deficit perspective interpret Fatima's withdrawal? How might this interpretation change when a teacher is attuned to equitable math teaching?
4. Ms. Morales and Ms. Bakir have a relationship where they can have respectful and difficult conversations. How does Ms. Morales respond to Ms. Bakir's concern? How could her response impact Fatima's confidence and math identity? How would you respond to Ms. Bakir and why?
5. Fatima's hijab is an outward statement of her religion, and being the only student wearing a hijab can feel isolating if negative stereotypes are prevalent in the community. How can Ms. Morales promote a more inclusive learning environment? How will promoting inclusivity impact Fatima's and her peers' math learning?

Case 4.3 Reframing and Valuing Student Voice

Ms. Cho, a first-grade teacher in a racially diverse classroom with multilingual students, is leading a whole-group math task on the concept of decomposing addends to benchmark ten as a strategy for addition. The task asks students to solve the problem: *Mary placed 7 pencils in one cup. Teidan added 5 pencils to the cup. How many pencils are there in the cup now?*

As Ms. Cho facilitates the discussion, she calls on Bo, who confidently says, "12."

Ms. Cho asks, "How do you know? Tell me how you figured it out."

Bo says, "Mary put pencils in the cup. Teidan put some pencils to make 10, and 2 more is 12."

Ms. Cho turns to Jamal to revoice Bo's strategy using the word "decompose" because Jamal typically uses the math vocabulary words that are discussed in class. She asks, "Jamal, can you explain what Bo just said using the vocabulary words we just learned?"

Jamal responds, "Bo decomposed the 5 into 3 and 2. He added 3 to 7 to make 10. Then, he added 2 more to get 12."

Pleased by Jamal's answer, Ms. Cho then says to the class, "Did you notice the word Jamal used? He said 'decomposed.' It's important that we all try to use our math words when we explain our thinking. That way, everyone can understand where the numbers came from."

Bo's shoulders began to slump as he leaned back into his chair, and he avoided eye contact with the class. Observing Bo's withdrawal, Ms. Cho realizes she highlighted Jamal's answer but did not validate Bo's original response. She tries to address her realization by saying to the class,

> "Math is about ideas, not just words. If I ask somebody to restate or add to your ideas, it's just because I think your ideas are important for everyone to learn from. Together, we can help one another say our great ideas using the math words we learned so that everyone in the class can understand."

For the next problem, Ms. Cho asks Bo if he can be the leader in developing a solution strategy for a word problem that could be solved by adding 7 and 8. Hesitant but encouraged by Ms. Cho's opportunity, he goes to the board and begins to solve the problem.

Bo says, "I got to do 7 plus 3 to make 10. So I got to break apart 8 into 3 and 5. Plus 7 and 3 for 10. Take 5 and 10 to get 15."

Ms. Cho pauses and addresses the class, "I want to take a moment to reflect on what Bo just shared. Bo showed us a brilliant way to think about this problem. He figured out how to benchmark 10 with the numbers, which is exactly what we've been learning. Now, let's work together to describe what Bo did using the math words we learned. Bo, would you like to try using the word "decompose" to explain your answer, or would you like some help?"

Bo nods hesitantly, and Ms. Cho calls on Xavier, who says, "Bruh, you decompose when you break apart."

Understanding what Xavier said, Bo responds with, "Okay, you decompose that 8 into 5 and 3."

Ms. Cho says, "Yes! That's it! Bo just used the word decompose to describe his strategy, and it was spot on. Thank you, Bo."

Reflection Questions

1 After Bo shares his first explanation, Ms. Cho calls on Jamal to revoice Bo's solution strategy using "decompose" to emphasize precise math language. How does Ms. Cho's instructional decision to publicly validate Jamal's response and not Bo's response devalue Bo's contribution? What is a different way Ms. Cho could have responded to recognize Bo's brilliance?

2 Ms. Cho realized that her decision had an impact on Bo. What did she do next to try to fix the issue?

3 Ms. Cho is focused on teaching the term "decompose" during the lesson. What do you think is more important: using math words accurately or the math thinking behind what words mean?

4 What are some strategies that you can use in your classroom to ensure students' use of math language while also highlighting the value of their math ideas?

Case 4.4 Math Is a Universal Language?

As a new fourth-grade math teacher at a diverse elementary school, Mr. Ronduen knew that his students spoke multiple home languages and would have differing English proficiency levels. He knew he needed to teach the math standards and address the English language development standards in his math lessons. Mr. Ronduen is a monolingual teacher, so he reached out to his colleagues for advice about teaching multilingual students.

A math teacher told him, "Students need to practice speaking in English to improve their communication skills. Mix up your groups so that they do not rely only on speaking in their home language. Besides, math is the easiest subject for them to practice speaking in English because it is a universal language."

This advice made sense to Mr. Ronduen since he has always heard that immersion is the best way to learn a new language. Mr. Ronduen took the advice to heart and purposefully mixed up the students to represent various home languages in each small group. He wanted students to work collaboratively, but they would have to speak in English to practice communicating in a common language.

Ceyda had just moved to the United States from Turkey before starting school in August. Her parents spoke and could read some English, but Ceyda had little exposure to the English language before moving. She did well academically in Turkey and loved math, but she was nervous about attending a school that only spoke English. Ceyda's parents assured her that there would be other children in the school who also spoke Turkish and that she would become friends with them.

Mr. Ronduen's school required teachers to follow a pacing guide for the math curriculum. The first unit he needed to teach focused on place value, extending from the hundredths place up to the hundred millions place (shown in Figure 4.1). Students were expected to use commas to separate large numbers into groups of three digits and to identify the groupings of whole numbers as ones, thousands, and millions. They also learned to use a decimal point to separate whole numbers from decimal

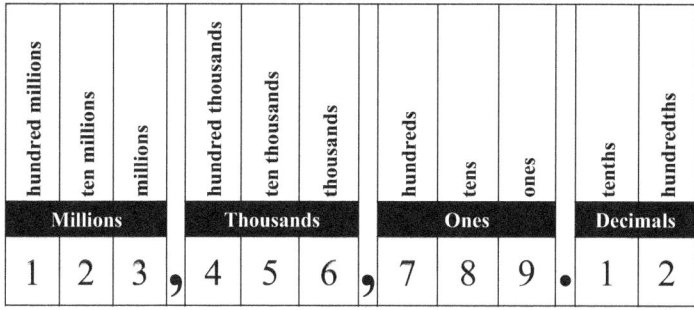

FIGURE 4.1 Example of a Place Value Chart with Notations from the United States.

fractions. Mr. Ronduen anticipated that teaching these notations would be relatively straightforward, requiring minimal explanation, as he assumed students already had prior experience using commas to separate the thousands group from the ones group. He also expected that students' familiarity with money notation would provide a helpful real-world connection to the decimal notation.

The lesson began with a review of students' understanding of place value within the thousands group. Mr. Ronduen instructed, "Let's practice writing numbers in standard form. Remember, standard form is the typical way numbers are written using digits. I will say a number aloud, and I want you to write it down." He then announced the first number, "Forty-three thousand, two hundred fifty-six." Speaking slowly, Mr. Ronduen repeated the number twice more to give students ample time to write it correctly and check their work. He encouraged collaboration by adding, "Show your paper to the members of your group. Did everyone write the same number? If not, discuss how it could be corrected."

Ceyda did not know what Mr. Ronduen asked the class to do, but she followed along with her classmates. She took out paper and pencil, but she was unsure what to write down. Her group members independently wrote their answers and quickly flashed their papers to one another, but Ceyda didn't get a good look.

Two students in the group said, "We got the same answer. Cool."

No one at her table spoke Turkish, so she couldn't ask them to let her see their paper for longer. She felt frustrated but determined not to give up. She waited until Mr. Ronduen asked a volunteer to write the number on the board. Citlali went to the board and wrote, "43256." Many students started nodding like they agreed, so Ceyda copied the digits on her paper. She knew those were too many digits to write without a separator, so Ceyda wrote "43.256" on her paper (see Figure 4.2 for more information). Ceyda already learned to use a period to separate large numbers during her math class in Turkey.

Mr. Ronduen asked if anyone wanted to add to Citlali's work, and Mohd added a comma between the 3 thousand and the 2 hundred. Ceyda looked at the board confused and wondered if this lesson was about decimals.

Mr. Ronduen then wrote a few numbers in standard form on the board and asked the students to write the numbers in word form. Since he knew there were many multilingual students in the class, Mr. Ronduen passed out a chart with the numbers and the spelling of the word form that would help the students. There were also some translation dictionaries available for students to use. Mr. Ronduen set a Turkish-to-English translation dictionary on Ceyda's desk and said, "This might help."

Ceyda wasn't sure what he said, but her parents had shown her how to use a translation dictionary before. She opened it up and translated the words on the number chart. She now

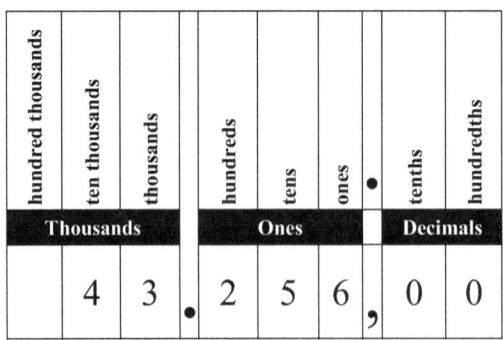

FIGURE 4.2 Example of a Place Value Chart with Notations from Turkey.

understood that this lesson was about place value, but she was confused about why Mr. Ronduen would teach the students wrong about how to write numbers. She decided to write the numbers in the way she had previously learned and quickly completed the task of writing the numbers in English.

For extra practice, Mr. Ronduen gave the groups a few more problems to work on together. He walked around to check on each group's progress, answer questions, and probe for deeper understanding. When he got to Ceyda's group, he noticed that she shared numbers with the group that used decimals to separate the groupings of three digits instead of commas.

Molli, Ceyda's group member, said, "Mr. Ronduen, are we supposed to use decimals or commas? Ceyda keeps using decimals. Maybe she was taught differently, but aren't numbers the same everywhere?"

Mr. Ronduen replied to Molli, "Numbers are the same everywhere." He knew Ceyda was still learning English, so he felt he needed to ease confusion in the group. To help Ceyda, he decided to model it for her by writing on her paper. He circled the decimals and said, "No. These are commas." Then, he wrote commas in their place.

Ceyda was surprised that her teacher was correcting her work for doing something wrong. She knew that she should never argue with a teacher, so she shook her head no and quietly said, "Hayir." Then, she decided to just give up on the task.

Reflection Questions

1 Math is often described as a universal language, just like Mr. Ronduen's statement that numbers are the same everywhere. How does this assumption create a confusing and frustrating experience for Ceyda, who was taught a different notation for writing large numbers?

2 Mr. Ronduen wanted students to write the standard form of a number, so he made the instructional decision to read the number aloud. How might his instructional decision create a barrier for some students to participate in the task?

3 Mr. Ronduen made an instructional decision to provide feedback to Ceyda by writing on her paper. What message did his instructional decision send to Ceyda about her math work and knowledge? What message did his instructional decision send to the other students who witnessed the interaction?
4 What support did Mr. Ronduen provide to his multilingual students to engage in the math lesson? Were these supports effective for the students? Why or why not?
5 Consider the advice given to Mr. Ronduen about grouping students. Why do you think this advice was given? When might it be appropriate to group students this way, and when might it not be appropriate?

Case 4.5 Building Math Confidence Through Asset-Based Language

Mr. Guyton's kindergarten classroom buzzed with excitement during math time. Today's lesson focused on understanding combinations that make ten using Unifix cubes. Students sat in small groups with containers of cubes, exploring different ways to make ten.

One student, Jay, eagerly raised his hand to share his solution: "I have 6 red cubes and 5 blue cubes, so that's 10!"

Instead of correcting him, Mr. Guyton smiled warmly. "Thank you for sharing your thinking, Jay! Let's all give a raised clap for Jay?" The students giggled and clapped their hands once over their heads. "Your brilliance is what we need to solve this problem," he added. "Let's work together as a team to see what Jay discovered. Take out 6 red cubes and 5 blue cubes to see if you have 10." Together, they used counting strategies to double-check his work.

Vera offered, "6 and 5 make 11. Maybe Jay has one extra cube?"

Mr. Guyton nodded. "I love how we're using our brains to help our friends. Jay, show us how you used the cubes to find your answer."

Without hesitation, Jay held up his cubes and said, "I have red and blue cubes."

Mr. Guyton probed, "Count the cubes for us." Jay started counting the red cubes first by pointing to each one as he said, "1, 2, 3, 4, 5, and 6. 6 red and 1, 2, 3, 4. Oh, 4 blue. 6 red and 4 blue is 10."

Mr. Guyton directs his attention to Charles and says, "Charles, tell us what Jay found out about his cubes."

Charles says, "Jay said 6 and 5. He counted again and said 6 and 4. It's OK to count again."

"Wonderful, Charles," said Mr. Guyton. He continued, "Let's give a raised clap for Charles." The students clapped their hands over their heads. "Charles, you said that Jay revised his answer when he counted again and figured out that there were only

4 blue cubes and 6 red cubes. Jay and Charles, give each other an air high five because your two fives make a perfect 10 observation! Now let's find some more combinations for making ten."

As Mr. Guyton asks students to turn and talk about the cubes they observe on their desks, Dr. Thompson, the school administrator, walks in to observe. She quietly took notes as the children moved between sharing and justifying their combinations. No one seemed nervous about making mistakes when they counted their combinations. In fact, several students proudly shared their combinations of Unifix cubes, confident that their classmates would help them refine their combinations if needed. When she asked one group why they felt safe to share their thinking, one child replied, "We are all friends, and we help our friends!"

Dr. Thompson was struck by how students were positioned as capable mathematicians. The classroom norms—thanking students for their contributions, affirming their brilliance, and collaboratively solving problems—fostered a culture of trust and deep thinking. Even students with emerging English skills or limited math vocabulary shared strategies using gestures or manipulatives, knowing their ideas would be valued.

After the visit, Dr. Thompson met with Mr. Guyton and asked if he would be willing to lead a professional learning session on creating math spaces that allow students to share their emerging ideas and encourage asset-based discourse. She noted, "Your classroom is a model. Our students need to hear more often that their thinking matters, even when they're still figuring it out."

Honored by Dr. Thompson's offer, Mr. Guyton gladly accepts and shares, "Students need to know their contributions matter. We can work together to examine ideas and problem-solving strategies without focusing on having to be right first. The collaboration helps everyone in the class, and they are really sweet kids who love helping their friends. I reinforce that helping friends is just as important as sharing ideas, and their confidence has grown so much."

Reflection Questions

1. How does Mr. Guyton use asset-based language to communicate and affirm students' math thinking, even when the answer is incorrect? How might his approach reshape students' perceptions of mistakes and learning in math?
2. In what ways do Mr. Guyton's students demonstrate confidence, agency, and ownership over their math ideas?
3. What specific classroom norms are evident in this case that help foster safe and collaborative student-to-student communication? What role do students play in reinforcing these norms?
4. How would you respond to someone who thinks Mr. Guyton is reinforcing "wrong" answers?
5. How can teachers intentionally model and affirm peer interactions? What sentence stems or discussion tools could help students respectfully challenge and build on each other's ideas?
6. What school-wide structures exist or could be implemented at your school to support the development of classrooms grounded in asset-based language and norms? What opportunities might exist for peer observation, modeling, or collaborative planning to extend this work across grade levels?

5

Cases About Math Instructional Pedagogies and Tasks

Many teachers have described math standards as being a mile wide and an inch deep. This means that they feel there are too many standards they need to rush through without enough time to go deep with the math to build a conceptual understanding. Sometimes, teachers are required to use a particular curriculum or pacing guide that they feel limits their autonomy to teach in the ways that are best for their students. Even through these constraints, teachers do have the power to decide how math lessons will be structured, the tasks students will engage in, and how students will demonstrate growth in their understanding of the math content. What math we choose for students to engage in or not engage in, and what that engagement looks like, are equity issues themselves.

The cases in this chapter present teachers' instructional decisions and math tasks they choose for their students to engage in when learning math content. Each case will provide some information on the content and the task, but the focus is on how students respond to the teachers' instructional decisions. As you read the following cases, examine how the teachers intentionally consider their students' identities and how this impacts the students' math learning. Also, examine when students' identities are not considered and the unintentional barriers that are then created for their math learning.

As you read and reflect on these cases, think about the math lessons you choose for your students to do. Are you following lesson plans that were given to you and are not based on your students' experiences and identities? Or do you modify your math lessons so that your students feel a sense of inclusion that builds positive math experiences? After reflecting on the cases, remember to go to Chapter 7 for additional points for consideration.

The following equity cases are included:

- *Case 5.1 Gender and Binary Story Problems* – Ms. Glen, a first-grade teacher with seven years of experience, faces an equity-related dilemma when a binary-gendered story problem unintentionally positions her nonbinary student, Sam, at the center of a classroom debate about gender. While Ms. Glen aims to build relatable math contexts, her preplanned lessons reveal assumptions about student identities and highlight the importance of creating inclusive tasks that affirm all students. This case invites reflection on how thoughtful, responsive planning and inclusive language can support both math understanding and students' sense of belonging.
- *Case 5.2 Using Technology to Practice Place Value* – Sra. Garcia, a second-grade teacher, introduces Dash robots to teach place value concepts, but she encounters equity issues when students with limited access to technology find it challenging to engage with the activity. While some students excel, others become passive participants, highlighting the importance of ensuring all students have equal access to technology and foundational skills. The case emphasizes the need for inclusive strategies and differentiated support when using technology in math instruction.
- *Case 5.3 Overcoming Roadblocks in a "Race to Mastery"* – Ms. Applegate, a third-grade teacher, designed a timed multiplication challenge and race-themed bulletin board to promote fluency. However, when a student named Emma, who enjoyed math and had strong agricultural knowledge, began to express anxiety and internalize

gendered beliefs about her math ability, Ms. Applegate recognized equity-related issues in how classroom norms were unintentionally reinforcing stereotypes and undermining confidence. Reflecting on these implications, she shifted toward more inclusive, culturally responsive strategies that honored students' real-world experiences, promoting deeper understanding and supporting positive math identities for all learners.

- *Case 5.4 Comparing Fractions in Safe Spaces with Number Talks* – Ms. Lee, a fifth-grade teacher, begins implementing number talks after participating in a school-wide professional development initiative aimed at promoting math discourse. While introducing the routine, she faces challenges related to classroom norms and equity, especially in supporting Adrian, a new student from Mexico who is hesitant to speak in front of the class due to language barriers and recent racist taunting from classmates. Ms. Lee uses number talks as a way to highlight Adrian's math strengths, setting the stage for a more inclusive classroom culture.
- *Case 5.5 Stuck in the Script* – Ms. Daniels, a third-grade teacher, teaches at a school that has district-adopted, scripted curricula. While teaching a word problem involving equal sharing division, she observes student frustration with the context of the problem. She begins to wonder what flexibility she might have in adapting the curriculum to design a problem that her students can better relate to while also ensuring that the lesson goals are preserved.

Case 5.1 Gender and Binary Story Problems

Ms. Glen has been a first-grade teacher for seven years and is confident in the content she teaches her students. Over the years, she has refined her lessons and preplanned her lesson plans for the entire school year, eliminating the need for weekly planning. Knowing that her lessons require minimal preparation, Ms. Glen often makes any necessary last-minute adjustments the morning of the lesson.

This year, Ms. Glen has a student in her class who does not identify as a boy or a girl. This student's name is Sam, and they are a social student who is typically eager to work on math tasks. Ms. Glen does not treat Sam any differently than their classmates besides allowing Sam to use the teacher's restroom. Ms. Glen also ensures she uses the correct pronouns for all students.

Ms. Glen knew that part-part-whole story problems can sometimes be challenging for students, as quantities in a story do not change but are described using different words to find the unknown quantity. In the past, she found the language demands for students learning English were distracting them from learning the math, so Ms. Glen refined her story problems to have two parts of a whole that she felt would be relatable to her students. The story problem she had ready to use is *Ms. Glen has _ students in her class. _ of the students are boys. How many students are girls?* This story problem often leads students to count the number of girls in the class, so Ms. Glen always asks her students to use two different strategies to explain the answer. To complete her lesson planning, Ms. Glen simply needed to update the class slides with the total number of students and the number of boys in the class. The recording sheets were already printed and ready to be used.

During the rush of the morning, Ms. Glen quickly counted the boys in the class and filled in the blanks on the class slides. She then called all the students to the carpet to introduce the story problem. Once the students were sitting quietly, she said, "Today I am going to read a new math story problem that I want you to help me solve. This story is about our class!"

The students smiled and wiggled in anticipation.

"I will read the story problem to you, and I want you to describe two different solution strategies. You will go to your table and independently work on solving the problem using one strategy, and then work with your group to find another strategy. How many strategies do you need to use to explain the answer?"

The students responded, "Two!" Ms. Glen said, "That's right. Now I will read the story problem to you. Ms. Glen has 21 students in her class." She pointed to all the students, and they smiled. She continued, "Twelve students in her class are boys. How many students are girls?"

Sam's smile immediately vanished as the other students looked around the room and began counting. One student raised his hand and yelled out, "Nine!" Another student said, "No, it's eight!" Then the class started debating the total number of girls in the class and whether Sam counted as a boy or a girl. Ms. Glen felt a sense of panic. She didn't mean to position Sam at the center of a debate about gender. She begins to wonder what she can do next to support Sam and the rest of the class in unpacking the context of the problem while also looking at the solution strategies shared.

Reflection Questions

1 Ms. Glen is teaching a lesson on part-part-whole story problems with one part unknown, which is typically found in first-grade math standards. Why is this story problem considered a part-part-whole one part unknown?
2 Why did Ms. Glen consider the story problem relevant to her students? What assumption(s) did Ms. Glen make about her students?
3 What was the impact of using a binary-gendered story problem?
4 Ms. Glen preplanned her lessons ahead of the school year. While this strategy can be effective, her plans were

not responsive to her current students. How can teachers plan lessons that are responsive to students ahead of the school year? What are some ideas teachers should consider?

5 Ms. Glen knows she positioned Sam in an uncomfortable situation. What advice would you give to Ms. Glen to guide her next steps and help repair her relationship with Sam?

6 Write a new part-part-whole one part unknown story problem that Ms. Glen could use that is more responsive to her students' diverse identities in the classroom. Describe how your story problem might be responsive to students' diverse identities.

Case 5.2 Using Technology to Practice Place Value

Sra. Garcia is a second-grade teacher in a predominantly Latinx elementary school where students come from various socioeconomic backgrounds. The school recently received a grant to introduce an educational technology tool (Dash robots) into their math curriculum to enhance students' engagement and understanding of math concepts through interactive and hands-on learning. Dash robots are small, interactive robots that use sensors to move directionally with programmed commands. Sra. Garcia wants to introduce the Dash robots to engage her students in an activity that allows them to practice identifying the place values of three-digit numbers and communicating the number's expanded form.

Sra. Garcia designed an activity requiring students to move the Dash robots on a floor grid to match the values of each digit in a three-digit number she would read aloud. She made number cards (0–9) to randomly pull to create the three-digit number students will reference. She also designed a program on the Blockly app (the coding program for Dash robots) that is downloaded to the students' tablets. Students will use Blockly to plan how the Dash robot will travel to each digit in the number Sra. Garcia shares with the class.

Students will start with the number in the hundreds digit and then move to the tens digit and the ones digit. They will also audio record the value of each digit so Dash can communicate the expanded form of the number as it travels across the floor grid. For instance, the Dash robot will start on the 3 in the hundreds place, play the recording "356 in expanded form equals 300 plus," travel forward 2 units, then turn right and travel forward 1 unit to move to the 5 in the tens place. The Dash robot will play the recording "50 plus" and continue to the 6 in the ones place.

Since the robot will move in different directions, turn, and play voice recordings, Sra. Garcia reserves a few minutes for a brief tutorial introducing students to the Blockly programming commands. She knows students are familiar with using technology outside of school, so she assumes they will apply their previous experiences using tablets and other educational toys to quickly adapt to using the Dash robots.

After students were randomly assigned into groups of four to engage in the activity and a brief introduction to the Dash robots was given, Sra. Garcia pulled the number cards for 263. After sharing the number with her students, she asked the groups to program Dash to identify and say the hundreds, tens, and ones of the expanded number. All the groups began working.

As she watched the students devise a plan and begin to program, she observed some students dominating the use of the Dash robots in their groups. For instance, Ana and Rafael, who frequently use tablets and coding games at home, quickly took charge. They could input commands efficiently and move the robot with minimal guidance. When the robot stops to say the expanded form, the Dash robot speaks using Rafael's voice since he is familiar with programming his voice recordings onto a tablet.

Conversely, their group members Maria and Nicolás, who had limited access to technology at home, struggled with programming Blockly and coding the robot to move to the next digit on the floor grid. Though they did identify the place values and the expanded form of the three-digit numbers, they often needed their peers to repeat the code and required additional time to understand how to control the robot. This developing understanding of technology led to frustration and decreased confidence in their abilities to contribute to the activity.

When Sra. Garcia walked around to assess the Dash robot's path and recordings after a few rounds of pulling cards, she saw Ana continuously take on the role of the "programmer" in the group as Rafael calculated the code and did the recordings for the robot. At the same time, Maria and Rafael were relegated to a passive role, merely observing without hands-on involvement.

Sra. Garcia was disappointed that the structure of the lesson didn't lead to shared participation. She wondered how she should use the Dash robots in the future.

Reflection Questions

1. How is the Dash robot being used in the activity to communicate students' understanding of the place value of a number in terms of the hundreds, tens, and ones? Is using the Dash robot an appropriate instructional strategy? Why or why not?
2. How could Sra. Garcia create a more inclusive learning environment to ensure all students have the foundational skills necessary to participate in meaningful math activities that use technology?
3. To help students reflect on how using Dash robots guided their understanding of place value, Sra. Garcia can ask questions that encourage deeper thinking about the process and concepts involved. What questions could Sra. Garcia ask during the activity to inquire about the process (e.g., programming steps, understanding movements) and reinforce the concept of place value (e.g., conceptual understanding, application of knowledge)?
4. How can teachers recognize and address the disparities in technological access and proficiency in their classrooms when integrating technology to support or enhance math learning?

Case 5.3 Overcoming Roadblocks in a "Race to Mastery"

Ms. Applegate teaches third grade at Oakville Elementary School, a K–5 school serving just over 250 students in the rural farming town of Oakville. The school reflects the deep-rooted traditions of the community and maintains a strong connection to agriculture. Many students at Oakville Elementary School bring practical skills and real-world knowledge from their families' agricultural work to their classrooms. Ms. Applegate recognizes these strengths and incorporates farming practices, animals, and nature into her math lessons to make learning more relevant and connected to students' experiences in problem-solving and caring for the land.

Early in the school year, Ms. Applegate introduced timed multiplication tests with the goal of helping students improve their speed and accuracy when multiplying. She would pass out the tests, set her classroom timer to three minutes, and tell her students, "Go!" To motivate her students during the timed tests, Ms. Applegate created a "Race to Mastery" bulletin board featuring a racetrack where students moved their race car icons based on their performance. The racetrack had a starting line, three checkpoints, and a finish line. Checkpoint 1 indicated mastery of the timed tests with the foundational facts 0s, 1s, 2s, 5s, and 10s. Checkpoint 2 noted mastery of timed tests with the facts 3s, 4s, and 6s, while Checkpoint 3 noted mastery with facts 7s, 8s, and 9s. The finish line indicated mastery of all of the multiplication facts within 10. Ms. Applegate envisioned this race track as an assessment tool for students to visualize their improvement and celebrate milestones as they master their multiplication facts. However, she noticed that many of her students did not respond as she had anticipated to the timed tests and the race track assessment tool.

When the timed test began, Ms. Applegate observed panic in some students' eyes. She noticed that Emma, a student who usually enjoyed math, often would not complete the timed tests and make many errors. Her car on the race track had hardly moved, so Ms. Applegate decided to talk with Emma to learn more about what was happening.

Emma said, "I get scared about the time and cannot think of the answer. I guess I am just not good at math like Justin, Evan, and Charles."

Ms. Applegate realized that those three boys were always the first to complete their timed tests and were the leaders on the racetrack. She said, "Don't worry about the boys. I want you to focus on your race car."

Emma replied, "What's the point? I'm not going to win anyway because boys are better at math. Everybody knows this!"

Ms. Applegate realized that Emma had formed an identity about herself as a girl learning math, and her view about herself is something other students might also think.

Ms. Applegate did not like how some students felt inadequate, especially when comparing themselves with the three boys who seemed to be crossing the checkpoints faster and "winning" the race. Furthermore, she grew concerned that the focus on speed overshadowed a deeper understanding of the math concepts. When considering math fluency and what it looked like, Ms. Applegate knew it was much more than calculating quickly. Fluency also requires flexibility and appropriate strategy selection, which Ms. Applegate notices is impossible to assess with timed tests. She questions her instructional approach and puts the timed test aside to try something different.

Ms. Applegate turned to inspiration from students' use of multiplication in their daily lives to stress flexibility and strategy selection. Like many of her peers, Emma came from a family with deep roots in Oakville's farming community. Through classroom conversations, Ms. Applegate learned that Emma loved horses and helped her family with various chores, like calculating feed ratios to determine how many buckets of feed to give to various animals.

Ms. Applegate encouraged Emma to think about multiplication like her farm chores. She asked Emma, "How many horses does one bale of hay feed?"

Emma responded with, "4 horses."

Ms. Applegate replied, "If you put out 3 bales of hay, how many horses could you feed?"

Emma quickly responded, "12!"

Ms. Applegate asked, "How do you know you could feed 12 horses with 3 bales of hay?"

Emma answered, "4, 4, and 4 is 12 total. I just quickly added them together."

Ms. Applegate then asked, "What multiplication fact is this like?"

Emma thought briefly and smiled brightly to say, "3 times 4!"

Ms. Applegate said, "Yes! You do multiplication every time you help feed your animals."

This strategy helped Emma see multiplication as combining groups of equal size. It also made her realize that she was doing math every day.

Ms. Applegate offered strategies for Emma to practice multiplication at home, such as relating the feed ratios to the multiplication facts they learned in class. She began associating the second factor in the multiplication problem as the multiplicand—the number being multiplied or the number of animals that can be fed per one unit of food. She also began associating the first factor as the multiplier—the number showing how many times the multiplicand is being counted or how many units of food would be put out for the animals.

Ms. Applegate used the planned time for the timed tests over the next few weeks to highlight ways her students use multiplication outside of school and share examples the students created to review related multiplication tables. As the students progressed in learning their multiplication tables, Ms. Applegate individually provided feedback to each student. She then took down the "Race to Mastery" bulletin board so as not to publicly display their progress to the class.

When it was Emma's turn to share how she uses multiplication, she said, "I use multiplication daily to feed the animals on my farm. This morning, I fed my chickens. One bucket of feed is enough for 8 chickens. If I used 4 buckets of feed, how many chickens did I feed in total?"

After her peers worked to solve the problem, Emma proudly shared her strategy of multiplying 8 × 4, which equals 32.

Reflection Questions

1 In what specific ways did Emma react to Ms. Applegate's "Race to Mastery" timed multiplication tests, and how might this approach have influenced her perception of gender stereotypes and her abilities in math? How do instructional methods like this shape students' broader identity and feelings of belongingness in math?

2 When Ms. Applegate began to question her "Race to Mastery" timed tests, what deeper implications or unintended messages might she have been reflecting on? How might these messages affect students' self-perception and learning experiences in math?

3 Why must teachers critique their instructional practices, especially when students show signs of disengagement or develop negative beliefs about their math abilities? How does such self-reflection shape the learning environment?

4 As Ms. Applegate sought to enhance fluency and build confidence in doing math, what specific instructional strategies did she attempt to modify? How did Emma respond to these changes, and in what ways did they affect her view of herself as a math learner? What does this reveal about the connection between teaching methods and student identity?

5 Ms. Applegate began incorporating students' community assets to connect their lived experiences with school-related math. How can you apply this strategy in your teaching to create more equitable and relevant learning experiences for your students? How might this approach reshape students' relationship with math and their academic growth?

6 In what ways do you identify with Ms. Applegate? What strategies do you use to help students improve fluency with multiplication? In what ways do these strategies influence students' perceptions of math and their own math identities?

Case 5.4 Comparing Fractions in Safe Spaces with Number Talks

Ms. Lee has taught fifth-grade math at her school for the past seven years. She recently finished a professional development led by her school's math coach on using number talks as part of their daily routine. The professional development is part of a school-wide initiative to deepen students' understanding of math with a focus on student discourse. During a number talk, the teacher poses a purposefully crafted problem for the class to solve using mental math strategies. Then, the teacher calls on students to share their solution strategies. Classmates are encouraged to engage in the conversation by agreeing with students' solution strategies, asking clarifying questions, and making comparisons across students' approaches. The teacher guides the discussion by recording the students' ideas for all to see, asking students to restate each other's thinking, and facilitating conversations about whether students agree or disagree with the solution strategies. Ms. Lee wants to begin incorporating number talks into her daily math lessons, but she is worried about some of the students' interactions with one another being respectful and productive.

Some recent instances of bullying occurred against a new student from Mexico. Adrian, the new student, moved to the United States with his family during the summer. Though he can speak English conversationally, Adrian gets nervous about speaking in front of the whole class and would rather speak in small group settings. A group of boys, led by Thomas, taunt Adrian by asking questions like, "Are you here legally?" and "Want to cut my lawn?" Ms. Lee and other teachers intervene to protect Adrian and reprimand the boys when they hear the taunting because they know the racist beliefs that guide those comments. Ms. Lee knows that Adrian has a strong math background, and she wants to reinforce the value he brings to their math class. She decides to use the number talks to publicly acknowledge Adrian's math contributions and hopefully help his classmates connect with him and his ideas.

Ms. Lee asked her students to compare two fractions for their first number talk. She introduced the task by saying, "Today we will do a number talk where I want you to compare two fractions without writing anything on paper. When you compare the fractions, I want you to figure out which one is greater and why it is greater."

Henry yells out, "But I need paper! Why can't I write?"

Ms. Lee responds, "I want you to use mental math strategies to find the answer so you will not write anything down. When you have an answer, do not yell it out. Instead, you will put your thumb up on your chest to let me know you are ready to share. Remember that I want you to explain how you found your answer."

She looks around the classroom and sees everyone looking at the board, so she decides to begin.

Ms. Lee writes $\frac{5}{8}$ and $\frac{6}{10}$ on the board and looks back at her students. Some students look confused, and others are thinking.

Ms. Lee says, "I will not start calling on anyone to share their ideas until I see everyone with their thumbs up. There is more than one way to compare these fractions, so try to find a second strategy if you already have one strategy."

Ms. Lee notices that students' thumbs are starting to go up, but Adrian's thumb is still not up. She wants to give Adrian and other students more wait time, so she says, "I want you to tell me if $\frac{5}{8}$ is greater than $\frac{6}{10}$, less than $\frac{6}{10}$, or equal to $\frac{6}{10}$ and explain how you know." She waits another 30 seconds and notices Adrian's thumb and a few more students' thumbs go up.

Ms. Lee asks, "Adrian, which fraction is greater?" A couple of the students in the class groan, and Ms. Lee gives them a stern look. Then she looks back at Adrian and gives an encouraging smile. Adrian points to $\frac{5}{8}$ on the board, and Ms. Lee asks the class, "Does anyone agree with Adrian that $\frac{5}{8}$ is greater than $\frac{6}{10}$?"

Many students in the room nod their heads yes. Ms. Lee looks back at Adrian and asks, while shrugging, "How do you know $\frac{5}{8}$ is greater than $\frac{6}{10}$?" Ms. Lee knows that Adrian does not like to speak in front of the whole class, so she offers him the dry-erase marker to show his thinking on the board. Adrian goes to the board and writes $\frac{1}{8} > \frac{1}{10}$.

A few classmates laugh again, and Thomas says, "He can't even read. That's not even the problem."

Instead of correcting Thomas, Ms. Lee elevates Adrian's status in the class by saying, "Let's talk about Adrian's strategy because he did some good math here!"

Thomas looks skeptical, but Ms. Lee continues by asking, "If we take $\frac{1}{8}$ away from $\frac{5}{8}$, how many eighths do we have left?"

Some students respond, "$\frac{4}{8}$"

Ms. Lee then writes $\frac{4}{8} + \frac{1}{8}$ under where Adrian wrote $\frac{1}{8}$ on the board. Then Ms. Lee asks, "If we take $\frac{1}{10}$ away from $\frac{6}{10}$, how many tenths do we have?"

More students respond, "$\frac{5}{10}$"

Ms. Lee writes $\frac{1}{10} + \frac{5}{10}$ underneath where Adrian wrote $\frac{1}{10}$. Then she says, "Notice that Adrian only compared $\frac{1}{8}$ and $\frac{1}{10}$. Why could he do that? Talk to the person next to you about why Adrian only needed to compare $\frac{1}{8}$ and $\frac{1}{10}$."

Thomas turned to Brett, saying, "It's easier just to multiply."

Brett replied, "I think Adrian's way is easier. $\frac{5}{10}$ and $\frac{4}{8}$ are equal to half, so I only need to compare the parts that are not equal. I don't even have to multiply."

Reflection Questions

1. Ms. Lee asks the class to practice applying Adrian's strategy to another set of fractions. What could be some possible fractions Ms. Lee could present to the class, and why?
2. How was racism shown in this classroom? What would your response be in this kind of situation?

3 Number talks, as an instructional strategy, require a classroom environment where students feel safe and comfortable sharing their ideas. What could Ms. Lee do to create this environment prior to introducing number talks?
4 How did Ms. Lee help Adrian share his math ideas with the class? What are some supports you offer or could offer in your classroom to ensure students have equitable access to engage in math?
5 How does Brett's reply to Thomas elevate Adrian's status among his peers and recognize his math contributions?

Case 5.5 Stuck in the Script

Ms. Daniels sat at her desk, flipping through the next day's math lesson from the district-adopted scripted curricula. As a third-grade teacher in a Title I school, she had been instructed to follow the curriculum with fidelity. The lesson introduced word problems involving equal sharing division, and the scripted problem read: *A group of 4 friends went to the carnival and bought a package of 10 ride tickets to share. If they share the tickets equally, how many tickets would each friend get, and how many would be left over?*

Ms. Daniels hesitated. Few of her students had ever been to a carnival. Many came from families with limited resources and lived in a neighborhood where such outings were rare or unfamiliar. She had seen before how word problems left her students confused and disengaged when full of unfamiliar settings, names, or assumptions about students' prior experiences. But with district leaders emphasizing pacing and fidelity to the script, Ms. Daniels worried about getting "off-track" if she changed the problem.

The next day, she gathered the class and projected the problem onto the board. Immediately, hands shot up.

"What's a carnival?" asked Malik.

Ashantee said, "I went to a carnival with my family in Ghana, and everyone wore masks for the street performance."

"Isn't a carnival like a circus?" added Jojo.

"Why would they share tickets? Do you have to pay to get on rides?" asked Aaliyah, confused.

Ms. Daniels tried to briefly explain by saying, "A carnival is a place with rides, like a fair. You usually need tickets to ride things, so the friends are sharing them equally."

But the confusion lingered. The class grew restless. Some students attempted the problem, but most struggled, not with the division but with understanding what they were solving. Frustration built.

"This doesn't make sense," mumbled Ashantee. "I don't get why they're doing this. Don't you dress up for a carnival and ride on floats in the parade? You don't need to pay tickets."

A few students sat quietly, pencils down, feeling defeated before even working through the math.

Ms. Daniels felt guilty for placing her students in this position. She had known the context might be inaccessible, and now the students were spending more time trying to visualize a scene than doing the math. Yet, she also felt trapped. The curriculum told her to teach this way. It offered no suggestions for adaptation and no alternative examples. She wondered, "Am I failing my students if I stick to the script? What happens if I don't?"

That afternoon, after the students had left, Ms. Daniels reflected on the lesson. Dividing 50 tickets among 8 children and then looking for how many tickets would be left was mathematically appropriate for her students. However, the delivery had missed the mark because the scenario didn't connect with her students' lived experiences.

She opened her planning journal and scribbled: *What if I replaced the carnival with something they know? Like dividing snacks for a classroom party? I could even bring in snacks and model with them. Would that still meet the lesson goal regarding equal sharing and remainders? How do I meet district expectations and the needs of my students? How can I make the curriculum work for us, not the other way around?*

Ms. Daniels sat back and considered the dilemma, torn between fidelity to a scripted resource and her responsibility to make learning meaningful for her students. She knew this wouldn't be the last time she faced this challenge, and she was ready to start exploring ways to teach with, not from, the curriculum.

Reflection Questions

1 What specific challenges did Ms. Daniels' students face when trying to solve the carnival word problem, and why do you think those challenges arose?

2 Ms. Daniels wanted to change the context to be dividing snacks for a classroom party. How does this context change the lesson goals regarding equal sharing and remainders?

3. How have your own students responded to math problems with unfamiliar or culturally distant contexts? What signs do you notice when students are disengaged or confused due to the context of a task?
4. What are the potential consequences, both positive and negative, of following a scripted curriculum without adaptation? When does fidelity become a barrier to equity? If modifications of the tasks are not allowed, what can be done to ensure students have the necessary background knowledge to successfully engage in the math content?
5. In your own practice, when have you felt pressure to stick to the curriculum? How did you handle that tension?
6. How can teachers advocate for the flexibility to adapt curriculum materials to better suit their students' needs? What support, from administration or colleagues, might help in doing this effectively?

6

Cases About Engaging Families and Communities in Math

Children will hold multiple identities, and these identities are formed through their experiences and interests. Let's first imagine how children's home lives influence their identity. Children's families will communicate expectations for behavior at home, which might include keeping their room clean, attending family functions, and showing love to their grandparents. When children meet these expectations, they might form identities like being well-behaved, being family-oriented, or bringing pride to the family. Families will also communicate expectations for learning, which will directly influence children's math identities. For example, imagine a grandfather baking cookies with his grandchildren. As they measure ingredients, the grandfather shows the grandchildren how to add fractional cups of flour and praises them for their accuracy and precision. Those grandchildren might begin to form positive identities about their math skills and want to continue building those skills with their grandfather.

Beyond children's immediate family, the community in which they belong will also impact how they see themselves. Community can be described by a location, social characteristics, or shared interests within a group. For instance, location could be related to the town or region a child lives in. A child might live in a community with immigrant families who speak different languages, who eat many different types of food, and celebrate different traditions and holidays. Maybe the child is very involved in an activity and is surrounded by others who are involved in the same activity. All these aspects of the children's community will send messages to children about their strengths, weaknesses, and the value of learning. These messages will be a source for how students develop their identities.

Students bring multiple, interconnected identities that shape their experiences both inside and outside the classroom. To support the development of positive math identities, our efforts must extend beyond the boundaries of the classroom and into students' families and communities. This chapter was included with that purpose in mind. The cases presented in this chapter highlight the importance of communication, partnerships, and advocacy between schools, students' families, and the broader communities in which schools are situated. As you read the following cases, consider the implicit and explicit messages children receive about their identities when learning math. Whose experiences and ways of thinking about math are valued and devalued?

When you read these cases, reflect on your own students' families and communities. How much do you know about them and leverage them in your own math instruction? How have you advocated for your students so their full identities can be seen, valued, and used to support the math learning for the whole class? For additional points to consider after reading the cases, please read Chapter 7.

The following equity cases are included:

♦ *Case 6.1 Supporting Multilingual Families with Math Content* – Mr. Green, a fifth-grade math teacher, hosts an open house to communicate expectations for the upcoming school year. Language supports are provided to multilingual families to aid discussions about concerns and how to best support children with math homework.
♦ *Case 6.2 Advocating Access to Extracurricular Math Activities* – Ms. Ramirez, a fourth-grade math teacher, attends a Math Family Night and witnesses an outside

organization that is recruiting students for after-school and summer math enrichment programs. She advocates for inclusion in the programming hosted by this organization so more students in her school can participate.
- *Case 6.3 Navigating Family Help with Homework* – Ms. Goyal, a second-grade teacher, receives a note from a parent about teaching her child the "right way" to subtract numbers. Ms. Goyal considers how to respond to the child and the parent in ways that respect the parent's math knowledge while also meeting her instructional goals of building a conceptual understanding of regrouping.
- *Case 6.4 Exploring Community Partnerships to Enhance Math Applications* – Ms. Carter, a third-grade teacher, reaches out to a member of the community to create a project that has practical applications of area and perimeter. The community member comes to the school, and students become interested in getting involved with the project outside of school.
- *Case 6.5 Flea Market Experience* – Macella and Nina are both kindergarten teachers who are invited to their students' flea market booth. These teachers witness their typically quiet students as outgoing and confident salespeople while helping their parents. One teacher picks up on their math knowledge and thinks of ways for the students to demonstrate that knowledge in the classroom.

Case 6.1 Supporting Multilingual Families with Math Content

Mr. Green has been a fifth-grade math teacher for 16 years at Longview Elementary, and he has strong beliefs about teaching and learning math. During Mr. Green's teaching tenure at Longview, the student population changed as new families moved into the area. The number of families whose home language is not English increased, and Mr. Green felt he was not as connected to his students' families as he used to be. Mr. Green is a native English speaker and has picked up some words in Spanish, but his knowledge of languages does not help much in communicating with all of his students' families. He knows that some of the math he will teach this year will be challenging, and he wants to ensure strong partnerships with the families to support students with assigned homework. Mr. Green has always believed in teaching students math with detailed directions. He is confident that if his students take diligent notes in class, then the students' families will have enough information to help as needed.

To build a strong school-to-home connection, Longview Elementary offers an open house at the beginning of the year for students and their families to meet teachers and learn classroom expectations for the school year. While many families attend this event, the teachers also record their meetings and post the videos on their class websites for families who cannot attend. Students will often attend with their families and translate when needed.

At the open house, Mr. Green shows a presentation with minimal words and lots of pictures to communicate his expectations visually so the families could follow along. He provides time for adults and students to translate as needed after he talks through each slide. When he gets to the slide about homework, one of the parents, Ms. Qutob, raises her hand. Mr. Green acknowledges her, and Ms. Qutob turns to her son Mustafa to ask her question in Arabic. Then Mustafa says, "My mom said that she had trouble helping me last year know how the teacher wants the math to be done. The math is different, and she doesn't know how to do it the same way."

A few people in the room start whispering and nodding in agreement. Mr. Green responds, "I will ensure everyone takes detailed notes during my instruction. Students will also have the textbook to help with any steps we learn during class."

Mustafa translates this information to his mom, and Ms. Qutob does not look pleased. She responds to her son, and he translates, "She said she tried that last year, and it was not always clear." A few more families in the room nod and agree they also had the same experience.

Ms. Udalor says, "Last year was hard because the math had to be done a certain way that I had never seen before. It made homework very frustrating, and I want to help my child. If my child comes home and does not understand, how can I help?"

Some translations are quietly whispered, and many of the families begin agreeing.

Mr. Green thinks about the families' concerns and comes up with a possible solution. He says, "I could make short video explanations and post them to our class website. You could see how I am solving the problems so you can make sense of the students' notes."

Ms. Udalor says, "How will you create your videos? Is it possible for you to try using something that will allow us to pick captions in our language?" Many families once again nod in agreement.

Mr. Green promises the families that he will look into software that will make the videos easily translated for their viewing. He is not sure what he will use yet, but he is hopeful that he will once again build a strong school-to-home connection with his students' families.

Reflection Questions

1 Even though Mr. Green does not speak multiple languages, how did he try to create an inclusive environment for his students and their families during the open house?

2 How do you ensure all your students' families are included during school events? How do you make sure they are included in homework?
3 Mr. Green came up with the solution to make videos of the strategies learned in class so families can view them at home. Whose problem-solving strategies are the focus in these math classes? How could Mr. Green be more inclusive with problem-solving strategies that the families might be familiar with?
4 Ms. Qutob and other parents are concerned that the math needs to be completed in a particular way that they are not familiar with. Barriers between pedagogies and strategies for conceptual understanding exist regardless of English proficiency. How have you communicated your math goals with your students' families?
5 Technology is ever-changing, and there are constantly new ways to help with translations. What technology do you know about for supporting multilingual families with videos?

Case 6.2 Advocating Access to Extracurricular Math Activities

Ms. Ramirez, a fourth-grade math teacher at Lakewood Elementary School, is a passionate advocate for equity in education. The school serves a diverse student population, with 70% of its students qualifying for free or reduced lunch and representing a wide variety of cultural and linguistic backgrounds. Each spring, the school offers a Math Family Night, inviting families to explore hands-on math activities designed by local community organizations while also learning about different program offerings. Lakewood Elementary understands the needs of their families, so they provide a flexible evening schedule with access to transportation to the Math Family Night. As a result, the event is well attended by students and their families.

This year, there is a table hosted by SparkMath Academy, a private organization offering off-site after-school math investigations and summer enrichment programs. Intrigued by the math games and interactive math manipulatives at the table, Ms. Ramirez visits to look into the program offerings and encourages her students and their families to do the same. When at the table, Ms. Ramirez notices English-only recruitment materials with images of predominantly white, middle-class children. The materials advertise an after-school program held once a week off-site for $200 a week and a three-week summer math camp for $1,500. Ms. Ramirez began to question the inclusivity of the program offerings by SparkMath Academy.

As the event continues, Ms. Ramirez notices many students and families gravitate toward SparkMath Academy's table with excitement, but their enthusiasm wanes when they learn more about the program offerings, including availability and cost. Several family members expressed their frustration to Ms. Ramirez, as she had initially directed her students to visit the table to learn about math enrichment and support opportunities. One grandmother said, "Dominick loves math, but it's too expensive!" Knowing how important such programs can be for students and their families, Ms. Ramirez devises a plan to see how she can advocate for the students and their families.

As the Math Family Night ends, Ms. Ramirez stops to talk with Mr. Williams, the director of SparkMath Academy. She shares her concern for student access to several programs.

Mr. Williams responds, "We figured students attending this Math Family Night would not include students in aftercare or working families who don't speak English, so we focused our efforts elsewhere."

Alarmed by this assumption, Ms. Ramirez wishes to draw attention to how the recruitment practices and program offerings are not inclusive to all students. She asks Mr. Williams if she could schedule a meeting with him to help him learn more about the school's demographics and students' families, highlighting the importance of equitable access to math opportunities. Although initially defensive, Mr. Williams welcomes the idea, as he sees the importance of ensuring SparkMath Academy provides enrichment to all students in the community.

The following month, Ms. Ramirez sees Mr. Williams facilitating math games with students in the school's library. He says to her, "I took your advice and am now offering an on-site afterschool program for students to explore math games. I have so many students enrolled and excited about doing math!"

Ms. Chen, who has a daughter in Ms. Ramirez's class, came over to Ms. Ramirez and Mr. Williams. She shares, "This is the first time my daughter has had a chance to join a program like this. The program works well for my work schedule and is affordable with families like mine on a tight budget. When finished with work, I can play a math game with my daughter before heading home from school. My daughter's already excited about playing a new math game next week!"

Reflection Questions

1 The feedback Ms. Ramirez gave to Mr. Williams surprised him and initially made him defensive. How might you have responded to her feedback?

2 Mr. Williams targeted his recruitment practices to a particular group of students who, from his perspective, would be more inclined to attend SparkMath Academy's

offerings. How do these recruitment practices unintentionally perpetuate inequities? What is the impact of excluding due to costs, language barriers, and assumptions about families' access and availability?
3 What are some changes that can be made to SparkMath Academy's recruitment practices and funding model so it can be more inclusive to the student population?
4 What impact do you think SparkMath Academy's on-site after-school program has on students' motivation and math learning? How might programs like these impact a student's math identity?
5 What math-related events are offered at your school or are available in your community? Are the events accessible to all students? If not, what can you do to advocate for inclusivity?

Case 6.3 Navigating Family Help with Homework

For the past two weeks, Ms. Goyal's second graders have been exploring place value, building two-digit numbers with Unifix cubes and base ten blocks. Today, Ms. Goyal asked the students to combine two addends on a place value chart using the Unifix cubes. The students enjoyed finding a group of 10 ones that could be grouped together by connecting 10 Unifix cubes into a tower. Then, they moved the tower to the tens place to demonstrate regrouping. But when they started subtracting, Ms. Goyal noticed that some students weren't regrouping correctly. Instead of moving a tower of 10 into the ones place, they were just removing individual cubes from the tens place without paying attention to the place value.

To help the students understand regrouping in a more concrete way before using a standard algorithm, Ms. Goyal decided to switch the base ten blocks. Base ten blocks have the units (little cubes) grouped into tens (rods), hundreds (flats), and thousands (little cubes), so students have to trade blocks as they regroup from one place value to the next. She had the students work in groups to solve 43–19. As they worked, she noticed that some students found alternative solutions that did not require regrouping. Maneesh, for example, removed one of the rods first. Then he removed the three little cubes and used his pencil to cross off six more little cubes on one of the rods (Figure 6.1). When Maneesh was asked what his answer was, he responded, "24. I have two rods and just these 4 little cubes to count."

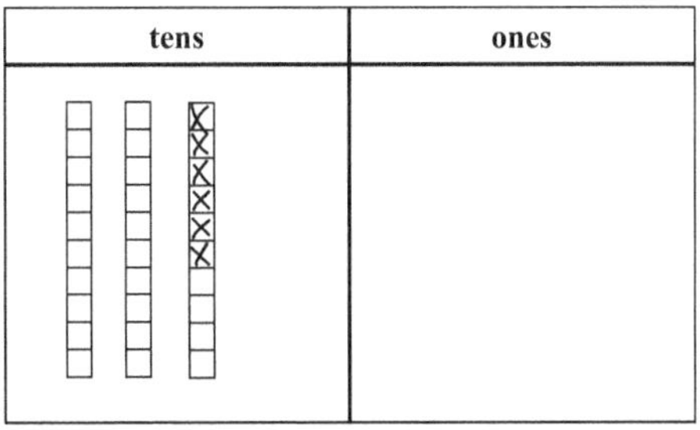

FIGURE 6.1 Maneesh's strategy to solve 43–19.

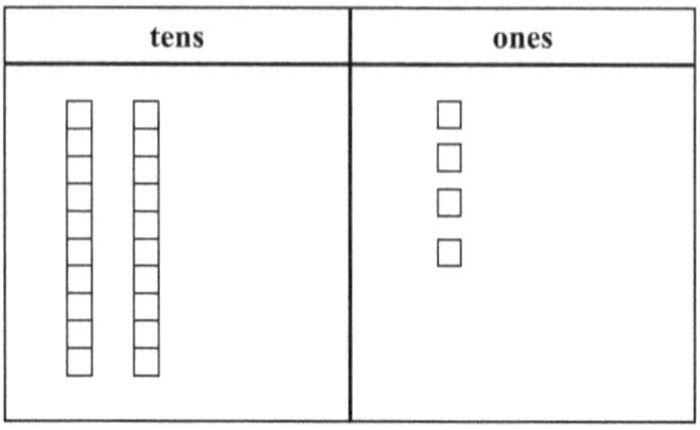

FIGURE 6.2 Isabella's strategy to solve 43–19.

Ms. Goyal saw this as a great teaching moment. She shared Maneesh's strategy with the class and then connected it to Isabella's approach, which involved trading a rod for 10 little cubes to subtract 9 ones (Figure 6.2). After a lively discussion, the students practiced Isabella's regrouping strategy with more two-digit subtraction problems. For homework, Ms. Goyal had the students work on additional subtraction problems that required regrouping. She even let them take home some base ten blocks so they could physically move the pieces when they practiced.

The next day, Ms. Goyal picked up the base ten blocks from the students and asked how they did on their homework.

Maneesh quickly said, "My mom taught me a new way!"

Ms. Goyal asked, "She taught you a new way with the blocks? Will you show me?"

Maneesh looked in his backpack and took out a paper. The paper had all the subtraction problems that were worked out using the U.S. standard algorithm for subtraction in the mom's handwriting. There was also a note that read: *Maneesh and I got confused with the blocks, so I showed him the right way.*

Ms. Goyal saw that Maneesh was excited to learn this new strategy, but she wanted the students to use manipulatives to regroup before they learned how to record the regrouping. The note about the "right way" upset her because it sounded like what she taught was somehow wrong. Other parents have praised her teaching because it helped students understand math better than just learning steps to calculate numbers. She gave Maneesh a smile and said, "Yesterday, you seemed to understand the blocks really well. What confused you when you got home?"

Maneesh replied, "I showed my mom my way and Isabella's way, but she said it took too long. That's why she taught me the new way."

Ms. Goyal asked, "Did you show her how the two strategies were similar?"

Maneesh replied, "I tried to, but I don't think she understood. But now I don't need to use the blocks!"

Clara overheard the conversation and said, "My dad was also confused about the blocks, but my older sister showed him how it works."

Then Carlos said, "I showed my abuelo, and he thought it was easy!" More students started to share their families' reactions to using the base ten blocks for subtraction.

Ms. Goyal did not want to undermine Maneesh's mom, so she walked away, wondering, "What should I do next? I know I should reach out to Maneesh's mom, but what do I say? How do I get families to understand that there is not one right way to do math? Also, how can I help them see the importance of building conceptual understanding?"

Reflection Questions

1. What does the "right way" imply about how Maneesh's mom is thinking about math? How might cultural differences in math instruction influence the strategies and methods families teach their children at home?
2. What could Ms. Goyal do next in this situation with Maneesh and his mom to build a positive and supportive relationship between school and home?
3. How could Ms. Goyal leverage Maneesh's new strategy in her review of using base ten blocks to subtract with regrouping? How have you incorporated a variety of solution strategies into lessons to validate diverse thinking?
4. The students describe many different reactions from their families about using base ten blocks to solve subtraction problems. How can Ms. Goyal communicate her math instructional goals with her students' families? How have you proactively communicated math strategies

and learning goals to students' families prior to possible misunderstandings?

5. Think about a time when a family member disagreed with you about how math was taught. How did you respond? Did your response build safe and respectful communication between the school and home? Explain strategies for how you might improve such communication.

Case 6.4 Exploring Community Partnerships to Enhance Math Applications

Ms. Carter, a third-grade teacher, has always sought to make math meaningful for her students. This year, she wants to integrate a service-learning approach by incorporating Indigenous knowledge and community voices into her math instruction. She decides to focus on area and perimeter, concepts that are essential in everyday applications. To make the lesson more relevant, she seeks to collaborate with a local Indigenous community member who can share insights into how math is used in traditional and contemporary ways within the community.

Recognizing that strong relationships are the foundation of meaningful collaborations, Ms. Carter begins by exploring connections within her classroom. She sends home a letter inviting families to share any knowledge or connections to local Indigenous groups. A student, Lily, excitedly shares that her grandfather, Mr. Redbird, is an artisan who builds traditional wooden structures for community events and gardens. He has extensive knowledge of measurements and works closely with the community garden next to the school.

Ms. Carter reaches out to Mr. Redbird through Lily's family, introducing her idea and inviting him to visit the classroom. She shared her goal of wanting to show students the real-world applications of area and perimeter while honoring Indigenous perspectives on land and traditions. Mr. Redbird agrees and suggests a project that will benefit both the students and the community.

During his classroom visit, Mr. Redbird shares with the students how Indigenous communities have long used math concepts to plan and build sustainable spaces. He explains how area and perimeter are used to design community gardens, ensuring that they make the most of available land while respecting the environment.

Tabria, a shy yet inquisitive student, shows great interest in Mr. Redbird's visit and his shared community knowledge. She asks, "Can we help you design a garden for your community? I want to give back by planting vegetables and flowers."

Mr. Redbird is intrigued by Tabria's idea and jumps into action. He says, "I know an empty plot of land measuring 10 ft by 12 ft that needs attention in the community garden next to the school. Let's work in small groups to design a space with two raised garden beds: one for vegetables and one for flowers. You need to decide how big each garden bed will be while making sure they both fit inside the plot of land."

As the students begin to work in their groups, Ms. Carter writes the task directions on the board from Mr. Redbird. She records the following:

Your Task:
1. Decide on the size of each garden bed. The vegetable bed should be a rectangular shape, and the flower bed should be a rectangular shape.
2. Find the area of each raised bed and make sure the total area doesn't exceed the area of the garden plot.
3. Find the perimeter of each raised bed to determine how much wood you need to build the beds.

As the students work, Mr. Redbird observes the excitement in the students' actions. Jay, who is in a group with Tabria, asks, "Mr. Redbird, will one of our designs actually be built? I want to visit and help build the beds. Can I make a sign that says, "Ms. Carter's Class" so everyone knows we helped?"

Excited by Jay's questions, Mr. Redbird shares, "I don't see why not. The community could use all the support we can get."

Tabria follows with, "Do you think we can also help you plan for what vegetables to plant? If we find vegetables that can help us share more food with the community, that would be pretty cool!"

Mr. Redbird gives a big smile. Ms. Carter nods at Mr. Redbird, saying, "Thank you for inspiring the students. Let's discuss how we can continue supporting the garden and the work you do for the community."

Reflection Questions

1 How did Ms. Carter facilitate an opportunity for community involvement in her classroom? What value does this bring to her classroom and the community?
2 How did the students respond to Mr. Redbird and make use of math to engage in real-life applications of area and perimeter? What about service and justice-oriented connections?
3 Considering Tabria's input, what is a potential follow-up question or activity that Mr. Redbird and Ms. Carter might jointly ask of the class?
4 What are some ways you can build community relationships in your context?

Case 6.5 Flea Market Experience

Macella and Nina are both kindergarten teachers who each have one of the Reyes twins in their classes. They both received an invitation from the Reyes family to come see their booth on Saturday at the local flea market. This flea market features vendors offering crafts, refurbished goods, services, and food, along with entertainment. Though neither of them had ever been to the flea market, they were excited to see the twins outside of school.

The Reyes twins, Camila and Elena, were quiet students who were having a hard time making friends with their classmates during the first month of school. They were most comfortable speaking Spanish with one another at lunch and during recess and would only speak in English when they were called on by one of their teachers. The kindergarten students would often hold each other to a high status when someone had light-up shoes, big bows in their hair, or a lunch box with the latest cartoon character. Camila and Elena's family did not buy them these things, so their peers often would not include them in play and learning activities.

When Macella and Nina arrived at the flea market, they were surprised by how large and active the place was. As they walked to the Reyes family's booth, Macella couldn't help but notice all the different crafts being sold, different foods being cooked, and different languages that were spoken. She was in awe of the diversity that she had not seen in other parts of town where she typically spent her weekends.

Macella saw a vendor selling treats and said, "We should get a churro!"

Nina replied, "That place doesn't look sanitary. We can get something to eat when we leave here."

Macella thought the vendor looked fine, but she shrugged her shoulders and kept walking to the Reyes family's booth.

At the Reyes family's booth, Macella and Nina were surprised to see Camila and Elena confidently at the center of attention. The girls were talking with customers in both English and Spanish, proudly explaining the items their family had for sale.

They collected customers' payments, brought the money to their parents, and returned with the correct change, clearly communicating how much had been given and how much was returned. Macella observed the girls move with ease, switching between languages and managing transactions smoothly. This confidence and fluency in a real-world setting stood in stark contrast to the quiet, hesitant demeanor the girls often displayed in the classroom. Macella left the booth wondering how she could help Camila and Elena bring that same sense of voice, pride, and participation into their learning at school.

Macella said to Nina, "Did you see that? The girls know how to identify coins and bills! We haven't talked about money in class, but we should set up a store in the class where they can practice buying and selling items. Camila and Elena would love that, and they might come out of their shells too!"

Nina looked skeptical and replied, "Money is a first-grade topic, not kindergarten. Besides, I don't know if what they are saying is even correct. I don't know Spanish."

Macella took some Spanish classes back when she was in high school, and she remembered some of the numbers. She knew the girls were accurate in identifying the money up to $20, so she responded, "Look at how the girls are interacting with the customers and their parents. Everyone is happy with the exchange, and the girls are identifying the bills correctly without the customers telling them how much was handed to them. Plus, listen when they speak English. They are saying the amounts correctly. The math these girls use is incredible! If we don't create a mini store in class, we could at least use the flea market context when we write some math story problems."

Nina said, "I guess, but I don't know if the other students will know what a flea market is."

Macella looked excited and said, "I know what we can do! Let's take some pictures with Camila and Elena around the flea market that we can use for our story problems. The pictures will show the class where the girls help their family on the weekends, and we can highlight the math that the girls already know. Maybe we can take pictures of some of the items their family sells, and the girls can help explain how much each cost."

Though Nina was still apprehensive, both teachers approached the parents with the idea. The parents and girls were very excited about this new project, and the girls showed the teachers all of their favorite places around the flea market.

Reflection Questions

1. Macella and Nina approached the flea market experience with different perspectives. How does each of their perspectives influence what they notice and how they interpret what they notice?
2. Camila and Elena demonstrate different behaviors while at school and while they are helping their family at the flea market. What factors influence their confidence in both settings?
3. Nina states that learning about money is not within the kindergarten math content. When, if ever, might it be appropriate to introduce concepts that are beyond the grade level standards?
4. Nina brings up the point that flea markets might not be a context that all the students in her class are familiar with. How does Macella consider building students' background knowledge of flea markets to engage in math? What have you done to build students' background knowledge of math in unfamiliar contexts?
5. What opportunities have you taken to engage with your students' lives and experiences outside of school (e.g., community events, family businesses, cultural celebrations)? How did those experiences shape your understanding of who your students are beyond the classroom?

7
Points for Consideration

As elementary math teachers, we constantly reflect on our teaching practices, including what works, what doesn't, and how we can better support our students. This chapter is designed to help you do just that by highlighting key takeaways from the cases in the previous chapters. These takeaways focus on both the math content and the equity-related themes that influence students' experiences in math class.

Whether you're reading this chapter on your own or using it as part of a professional learning discussion, you'll find insights to deepen your understanding of the challenges and opportunities presented in each case. For facilitators, these highlighted issues can serve as discussion starters, helping to unpack the nuances of each classroom scenario. For individual readers, they offer new perspectives that can support your ongoing learning and reflection.

In Chapter 2, you explored the Equity Literacy Framework (Gorski & Pothini, 2024; Gorksi & Swalwell, 2015). The framework prompted you to consider the need for critical awareness and the associated skills required to recognize, respond to, and redress inequities in educational settings. Then, we looked at Louie et al.'s (2021) FAIR Framework, which helps us critically examine how access, identity, power, and recognition play out in math classrooms. Now, we'll take a closer look at how these equity-focused themes emerge in the cases. We'll also highlight key math content takeaways, helping you think not just about what is being taught but how it is being taught and how students are experiencing it.

As you read through the takeaways, we encourage you to consider how these insights connect to your own classroom. What practices do you already use that support equitable and effective math learning? What areas might you rethink or refine? And how can you create a math learning environment where all students see themselves as capable and confident mathematicians?

While we suggest our key takeaways, we also invite you to come up with more ideas on your own and expand on the ideas to lead critical conversations about equity. Now, let's dive in and explore these cases together.

CHAPTER 3 POINTS FOR CONSIDERATION

Cases About Math Classroom Community Norms, Policies, and Procedures

Case 3.1 First-Year Classroom Management

Many first-year teachers enter the classroom believing that strict rules and structured procedures will create an effective learning environment. However, rigid classroom management can sometimes do more harm than good, stifling student engagement and discouraging collaboration. In this case, a new kindergarten teacher enforces strict expectations to maintain control, limiting students' opportunities to interact, ask questions, and engage meaningfully with math. When a young student struggles to complete a worksheet, the teacher's approach leads to embarrassment and frustration rather than support and learning.

This case highlights the challenges teachers often face in balancing structure with flexibility and the unintended equity issues that can arise from well-intentioned classroom policies. When students fear making mistakes or feel isolated in their learning, their confidence in math, and in themselves, can suffer. By reflecting on how classroom norms impact student engagement and identity, teachers can create spaces where all learners feel valued, supported, and empowered to explore math thinking.

We highlight the key points for consideration from the case as follows:

1. *Building Conceptual Understanding Instead of Rote Procedures*
   In this case, students are asked to follow a procedure to fill in a worksheet where students write numbers starting at zero. Charles is confused by the procedure for completing the assignment for a couple of different reasons. First, when children learn to count they begin counting starting at one and not zero. For a kindergarten student who

is still learning the counting sequence, the directions for the assignment do not follow the counting numbers that begin at one. Second, Ms. Floyd's directions for filling in blanks on an equation made no connections to what it means to find number combinations that make a group of ten, which is the goal of the lesson. When we have students follow procedures without understanding in math lessons, all we do is teach them to follow directions and not actually teach them the math content. Number combinations for making ten is a fundamental math skill that will continuously be leveraged throughout elementary school when calculating numbers. It is essential for early elementary teachers to provide students with ample opportunities to build a conceptual understanding of this concept using manipulatives and pictures so they can visualize number combinations that make ten. The visuals can later be connected to equations so that students can draw from their previous experiences to learn abstract ways of representing quantities. Remember that rushing through concepts in math will not save time in the long run since reteaching will need to occur.

2. *Fostering Active Student Engagement in Math Learning*

Ms. Floyd's students were passive recipients of instruction rather than active participants in constructing knowledge. While lessons using worksheets can serve as a helpful tool to practice math skills, students need varied learning experiences that encourage them to explore math beyond procedural and rote instruction. To enhance engagement, lessons should incorporate discussions, games, manipulatives, and inquiry-based activities that encourage students to develop a deeper understanding of how numbers work together to make ten. Such lessons can contribute to equitable math classrooms that create learning environments where students feel safe and comfortable making mistakes and sharing ideas. When teachers create this type of classroom environment, students' engagement and confidence as math learners can increase.

3. *Shaping Math Identity and Student Perceptions*

   The way math is taught influences students' beliefs about their abilities. Ms. Floyd's rigid instructional approach and public reprimands reinforce a fixed mindset about who is "good" at math. Penalizing students for seeking help discourages perseverance and participation. Charles's negative learning experience may discourage him from participating in future math discussions. A more supportive learning environment where mistakes and questions are valued as learning opportunities can help all students see themselves as capable math learners.

Case 3.2 Differing Perspectives on Teaching Math Word Problems

When a teacher joins a new grade-level team, they often bring fresh ideas, especially if they've seen success with students in previous years. But what happens when those ideas clash with long-standing practices? This case explores the tensions that arise when a third-grade team insists on using a keyword strategy for solving word problems, while a new team member questions whether it truly helps students, particularly multilingual learners, develop strong problem-solving skills.

While a keyword problem-solving strategy is featured, the heart of the case addresses broader issues of instructional consistency, school policies, and deficit-based views of students' abilities. For instance: How do teachers navigate team dynamics when they see an opportunity for change? What happens when a strategy prioritizes quick answers over deep understanding? And, how can educators advocate for equitable practices that support all students in making sense of math?

We highlight the key points for consideration from the case as follows:

1. *Teaching Math Word Problems as Comprehension, Not Just Identification*

The CUBES strategy has been taught to students as a tool for solving math word problems. CUBES is an acronym for the following steps:

- **C**ircle the numbers: Identify and circle all the numbers in the problem.
- **U**nderline the question: Underline the part of the problem that asks you what to solve.
- **B**ox the keywords: Box or highlight keywords that indicate important details or operations.
- **E**liminate extra information: Remove any information that isn't necessary for solving the problem.
- **S**olve the problem: Use the remaining essential information to problem-solve a solution.

This strategy does not fully address the deeper reading comprehension needed for making sense of math word problems since it relies on surface-level identification of numbers and keywords. Many students will get in the habit of quickly identifying the keywords, selecting numbers, and calculating to find an answer without considering the reasonableness of the strategy. Keyword strategies, like CUBES, reinforce the belief that math is about shortcuts and tricks rather than comprehension. These strategies also do not work when there are no keywords present or if it is a multistep problem. Effective instruction should guide students in making sense of word problems rather than just identifying numbers and keywords.

Keyword strategies can also be especially problematic for multilingual learners. Math word problems do not always follow predictable language patterns, and keywords may not always indicate the correct operation. Instead, many teachers advocate for strategies that emphasize comprehension reasoning and problem-solving rather than surface-level identification of words and numbers.

2. *Supporting Multilingual Learners in Solving Word Problems*

Leticia's approach to solving word problems recognizes the importance of reading comprehension, particularly for multilingual learners, to engage in math conceptually. Strategies like using visuals, encouraging student explanations, and incorporating discussion can support deeper understanding. Furthermore, integrating literacy strategies, such as rereading, visualizing, and discussing problems, can be helpful for students to understand the context before solving. While these strategies are important to consider, it is equally important to ensure that the strategies do not lend to "easier" work that reduces math learning, which is not equitable. Making the math easier instead of making the language demands easier often suggests that multilingual learners are not capable. These lower expectations impact their overall access to high-quality math instruction.

3. *Supporting Meaningful Learning So All Students Can Engage*

    The assumption that students cannot engage in meaningful problem-solving due to low reading levels reinforces a deficit perspective. Instead of assuming students will struggle with word problems, teachers can scaffold comprehension by incorporating multilingual supports, peer discussions, and real-world contexts. Teachers should have the flexibility to introduce multiple strategies that help all students, particularly multilingual learners, develop conceptual understanding. Thus, a rigid adherence to the CUBES strategy may limit flexibility in instruction. By encouraging discussion and exploration of word problems, students can develop confidence and ownership of their learning.

4. *Balancing Instructional Consistency with Valuing Students' Math Identities*

    The belief that multilingual learners cannot engage with word problems unless simplified to a set of keywords undermines their math potential. Instead of reducing problems to isolated terms, encouraging problem-solving discussions and validating students' reasoning helps build their confidence as capable math learners. However, fostering this kind of rich, student-centered instruction can be challenging within rigid systems. The school's requirement for consistency across classrooms should not come at the expense of effective teaching practices. Leticia's challenge in advocating for change highlights the importance of collaboration among teachers and support from school leaders in making instructional decisions that truly benefit all students.

Case 3.3 Managing Manipulatives to Avoid Mishap

Managing classroom resources fairly while maintaining structure is a challenge many teachers face, especially when working with students who have diverse learning needs. In this case, a second-grade teacher grapples with how to distribute math manipulatives equitably, influenced by past teacher perceptions and concerns about classroom management. By restricting access to only a few students, she unintentionally limits hands-on learning opportunities for those who might benefit the most, including students with individualized educational programs (IEPs) and physical disabilities. This case raises important questions about implicit biases, inclusive teaching practices, and how educators can create policies that support both structure and equity in the classroom.

We highlight the key takeaways from the case as follows:

1. *The Importance of Hands-On Manipulatives for Learning in Place Value Instruction*

    The use of manipulatives is a powerful instructional strategy that can significantly deepen students' math understanding, particularly in teaching foundational concepts like place value. For young learners, who are still developing abstract reasoning skills, hands-on materials provide concrete representations of math ideas, making the invisible visible. By physically manipulating objects, students can explore number relationships, recognize patterns, and construct meaning through active engagement. When access to manipulatives is removed or restricted, it can unintentionally create barriers to learning by forcing students to rely on symbolic representations before they are developmentally ready, which may lead to surface-level understanding or misconceptions. Recognizing this, Ms. Baker encourages Ms. Fisher to incorporate base ten blocks into her instruction. These manipulatives offer a clear and consistent model of the base ten system, with units (ones), rods (tens), and flats (hundreds). This fixed structure supports students in visualizing and internalizing the process of regrouping, which is an essential component of addition and subtraction with multidigit numbers. Unlike Unifix or snap cubes, which can be rearranged in various configurations and do not inherently convey place value, base ten blocks reinforce the hierarchical nature of our base ten number system. Their design helps students make sense of how numbers are composed and decomposed, building a strong foundation for future work with algorithms, estimation, and problem-solving.

2. *Adapting Manipulatives for Individual Needs in an Inclusive Learning Environment*

   Ms. Fisher understands that in order to create an inclusive learning environment, it is essential to adapt instructional materials, such as manipulatives, to meet the diverse needs of all learners. For students like Amina, who may experience physical disabilities that make traditional manipulatives difficult to use, alternative tools can provide meaningful access to the same math concepts. Collaborating with specialists, such as special education teachers and paraprofessionals, can help identify and implement accommodations that promote full participation. This might include larger, easier-to-grasp base ten blocks, tactile or textured manipulatives, or virtual tools that allow for drag-and-drop interactions with auditory or visual feedback. Providing these alternatives not only supports individual needs but also affirms every student's right to access high-quality math instruction.

   At the same time, Ms. Fisher's classroom policy of designating only a few students as "Material Leaders" may inadvertently limit other students' opportunities to engage in active learning. While leadership roles can foster responsibility and classroom community, rigid restrictions on who can engage with materials may disproportionately affect students who benefit most from hands-on learning. For students developing conceptual understanding, particularly those with IEPs, English learners, or students who simply learn best through tactile experiences, limiting access can create barriers rather than scaffolds. A more flexible system, such as rotating the Material Leader role, establishing clear expectations for manipulative use, or integrating structured turn-taking routines, can ensure that all students have equitable access to learning tools without compromising classroom management.

Melvin's needs further highlight the importance of individualized support. His IEP clearly states a need for manipulatives, yet his access has been limited due to concerns about his behavior. Rather than removing essential supports, a more inclusive approach would involve implementing proactive strategies that ensure both Melvin's engagement and classroom safety. Structured routines and positive behavior reinforcement can help Melvin meet expectations while still accessing the tools he needs to thrive mathematically. By prioritizing flexibility, collaboration, and student-centered support, Ms. Fisher can cultivate a math classroom that values diversity and empowers all learners to participate meaningfully.

3. *Centering Students' Math Identities and Contributions*

Valuing students' contributions and nurturing their math identities is essential for fostering a classroom environment where all learners feel seen, heard, and capable. When students like Amina and Melvin express interest in engaging with manipulatives, their voices should be honored and not dismissed due to implicit biases or assumptions about their ability to engage with materials appropriately. Decisions rooted in these biases can unintentionally marginalize students, sending subtle messages about who is trusted, who belongs, and who is perceived as capable in the math classroom. To counteract this, offering all students the opportunity to take on leadership roles, such as managing materials or facilitating group work, can affirm their sense of agency and math competence. These roles not only build responsibility but also provide students with the chance to shape their learning environment and see themselves as valued contributors to the classroom community.

Additionally, it is important to consider how rigid classroom structures, such as overly strict rules around material use, can stifle collaboration and limit students' ability to support one another. This is evident when Amina's group members feel restricted by procedures that prioritize compliance over communication and flexibility. In contrast, classrooms that foster meaningful collaboration invite students to listen to one another's ideas, negotiate different strategies, and build collective understanding. To cultivate such an environment, it is critical for teachers to seek and reflect on student feedback regarding their experiences in math. Asking students what helps them learn, how they feel during group work, or what roles make them feel empowered can uncover valuable insights and reshape classroom norms to be more inclusive. When students feel that their voices matter, they are more likely to take risks, engage deeply, and view themselves as capable mathematicians with something important to contribute.

Case 3.4 One Teacher's Push for Inclusive Policies Beyond the Classroom

Many teachers face the challenge of designing homework policies that support all students, especially when families have diverse cultural, linguistic, and economic backgrounds. In this case, Mr. Moss grapples with language differences, limited access to resources, and rigid school policies that may unintentionally disadvantage some students. By seeking support from colleagues, connecting families to community resources, and offering more flexible assignment structures, Mr. Moss works toward creating a more inclusive learning environment. This case highlights the importance of questioning traditional policies, recognizing hidden inequities, and making small but meaningful changes to ensure all students have a fair chance to succeed.

We highlight the key takeaways from the case as follows:

1. *Math Understanding and Access*

    The case emphasizes the importance of ensuring all students can engage meaningfully with math content, particularly division concepts. Without appropriate support, students may struggle with comprehension due to language barriers, lack of resources, or limited family support in math problem-solving. Teachers can implement multiple representations of math ideas (e.g., visuals, manipulatives, real-world applications) to make division concepts accessible to all students.

2. *Linguistic Equity and Family Engagement*

    This case explores how language barriers can significantly impact student engagement and success in math, especially when students and their families face challenges understanding assignment expectations or classroom routines. When instructions and communications are only available in one language, it can unintentionally exclude families who are eager to support their children but are not fluent in the language of instruction. To bridge these gaps, educators like Mr. Moss can take proactive steps, such as providing assignment instructions in multiple languages, incorporating visuals or step-by-step diagrams, and partnering with bilingual family liaisons or translation services. These inclusive strategies not only improve access but also communicate respect for students' home languages and cultures. Importantly, family engagement should be viewed as an asset, not a deficit. Even when caregivers may not speak the dominant language, they bring valuable insights, cultural knowledge, and a deep investment in their child's learning. Honoring

these strengths helps build trust and a shared commitment to student success.
3. *Rethinking Homework Policies Considering Socioeconomic and Resource Barriers*

    Differences in students' home environments, such as access to quiet study spaces, technology, and materials, can create inequities when it comes to completing assignments. Traditional homework expectations often assume that all students have equal access to these resources outside of school, which can disadvantage those who do not. To address this, a more equitable approach would include providing classroom resources like supply-sharing stations and flexible due dates, as well as offering alternative ways for students to demonstrate learning, such as through peer study groups or community tutoring programs. By adjusting these practices, teachers can better support students without penalizing them for external factors. Moreover, teachers can advocate for changes in school policies to ensure that all students have fair access to the resources and opportunities needed to succeed.

4. *Teacher Advocacy and Systemic Change*

    Mr. Moss's efforts reflect the powerful role of teachers as advocates for equity. Rather than accepting rigid school policies or norms that may unintentionally disadvantage students from culturally, linguistically, or economically diverse backgrounds, he actively questions these practices and seeks solutions. By collaborating with colleagues, documenting barriers, and sharing student-centered recommendations with administrators, teachers can initiate systemic change that extends beyond their own classrooms. Simple but thoughtful adjustments, such as modifying assignment deadlines, offering alternative formats, or incorporating family-friendly communication methods, can model what equity looks like in action. When these classroom-level shifts are embraced school-wide, they can lead to more inclusive policies that ensure every student, regardless of background, has the opportunity to thrive. Ultimately, this case illustrates that equity work is both relational and structural, requiring empathy, intentionality, and ongoing advocacy.

Case 3.5 Identifying Students for the Gifted Program

Gifted programs face significant equity issues. Identification and assessment are not standard and can lead to policies that overlook the talents of students from marginalized groups. It is well documented that low-income, Black, and Latinx students are underrepresented in gifted programs, particularly when universal screening is not the norm. Reliance on teacher recommendations can lead to decisions being made based on biases of traditional views of what being "good at math" looks like instead of true giftedness. Over time, students who are a part of the gifted program will often be exposed to more challenging math curriculum, which will set them up to take more advanced classes that will prepare them for higher education and different career trajectories. Identifying with gifted programs can have lasting effects on students' math learning, so it is essential that policies are in place to combat the equity issues that can arise.

Ms. Davis notices that her fifth-grade student, Jamari, is disengaged and might not be challenged in his math learning. Since she recently completed a gifted certification, she decides to change up how she typically teaches her math lessons. When Jamari exhibits more engagement and leadership with the math lesson, Ms. Davis begins to question Jamari's previous teachers about why they never recommended that he be tested for the gifted program. This case highlights the importance of examining policies that rely on teacher recommendations that could be made based on biases.

We highlight the key points for consideration from the case as follows:

1. *Biases Related to Race*
   Black boys, like Jamari, are too often described with deficit terms like "distracted" or "troublemaker," even when they exhibit the same mirrored behaviors as other students in the class. The biases toward Black students

are demonstrated through the overrepresentation in school disciplinary systems and special education, while they are often underrepresented in gifted programs and advanced classes. How Black students are treated in schools can be traced to racism and negative stereotypes. To support the academic and well-being of Black students, it is essential to understand their lived experiences in the school system. By doing so, you can actively confront and work to dismantle the biases that exist within the school system and among school personnel.

2. *Biases Related to Math*

    Some people might think that math is just about numbers, but biases related to math can have a significant impact on students' access to high-quality math instruction. In this case, Ms. Davis changed her math instruction from one in which she would teach a skill and then have the students practice that skill multiple times. This type of instruction that focuses on one strategy is often prevalent in math classes, and it prioritizes following procedures for a preferred strategy rather than inviting creative approaches. Students could be good at following directions and score well on assignments that reinforce recursive practice, but they may have little understanding of the math behind the steps they are following. Students, like Jamari, could also find these types of assignments to be repetitive and boring. However, this approach is still a common method of teaching math. When teachers have a bias about what it means to be successful in math, like completing tasks quickly the way the teacher prefers them to be done, then they are less likely to provide opportunities for students to demonstrate their math strengths in other ways. How do you think students might engage in exploring the math concepts, and what experiences led you to think this way?

3. *Advocating for Universal Screening for the Gifted Program*

    Each school system has a different policy for how students are identified for the gifted program. Identification that relies on teachers' recommendations is subject to teachers' biases interfering with their decision-making.

Additionally, identification relying on out-of-school referrals by families or other professionals for gifted testing can present inequities in learning about the referral process. Families' home languages might not be considered in school communications. Also, schools that rely on their websites to communicate information might isolate families who do not have access to computers or the internet. To ensure that all students have the opportunity to be tested and identified for the gifted program, there must be universal screenings put into place. Teachers, parents, and caregivers need to advocate for this change if it is not already in place. If your school does not offer universal screenings for the gifted program, then make sure you advocate for students by recommending them for testing and personally reaching out to students' families so they can also advocate for testing.

CHAPTER 4 POINTS FOR CONSIDERATION

Cases About Communication in Math Classrooms

Case 4.1 Verbal and Nonverbal Communication

With limited time to cover content, teachers will often call on students who will help progress the lesson. However, this instructional practice could lead to the same students being called on multiple times and discourage other students from participating. In this case, a kindergarten teacher calls on the same students to share their answers with the class and chooses not to call on a nonverbal student to share with the whole class. The teacher's intention is to not single out the student by having them respond verbally in front of the class. With the insight of a paraprofessional, the teacher learns how to include all students in class discussions with a variety of ways to share their thinking. This case highlights the importance of inclusive classrooms where teachers intentionally plan for students to communicate math ideas in meaningful ways that meet students' individual needs.

We highlight the key points for consideration from the case as follows:

1. *Trusting Students to Go Deep with the Math Content*
    Part of equitable math teaching is going deep with the math that is taught, which requires teachers to trust that their students can learn content that may not be in the standards. Math standards vary from state to state and from country to country, which means that the content standards themselves should not limit what students have access to learning. In this case, a kindergarten teacher wants students to pay attention to defining attributes. To do this, she shows students pictures of a rhombus, trapezoid, and a square. Though the students are not introduced to these geometric vocabulary words, they do count the number of sides and determine that all

the shapes have four sides. With this concrete visual, the teacher introduces the word *quadrilateral* and provides a basic definition of having four sides. Though the geometric vocabulary word *quadrilateral* might not show up in the kindergarten math standards, it is appropriate to introduce students to this word within this context since they have models to make connections to. Students are capable of learning new words that teachers introduce them to, so do not be afraid to use appropriate math vocabulary.

2. *Planning for Communication Modalities*

   A lot of emphasis is put on verbal communication in math education. However, a focus on verbal communication alienates students who are nonverbal, those who are working toward English language proficiency, and even those who are shy. Teachers need to find ways to allow students to communicate using gestures, pictures, models, and even their home language as needed to demonstrate their math thinking. When provided with opportunities to use nonverbal forms of communication, students can feel like they are an essential part of the classroom community, and teachers can gain so much more evidence about their students' math understanding. Teachers need to be thoughtful in planning for multiple modalities of communication so students have authentic ways of participating in class discussions.

3. *Communicating Expectations*

   Teachers constantly communicate their expectations to their students through the instructional decisions they make. Ms. Patel tended to call on the same students whom she assumed had the "right" answer. Biases related to how students communicate, how math "should" be done, and more could be working behind the scenes that make teachers decide who will have the "right" answer and who will not. Only calling on certain students is the type of instructional decision that sends a clear message to students about who the teacher thinks is capable of doing math and who the teacher does not think is capable

of doing math. Students will internalize these faulty and biased messages as their own math identity. Teachers must constantly check their own biases and instructional strategies to ensure they are communicating messages that build positive math identities for their students.
4. *Building Critical Friendships with Colleagues*

    The relationship between Ms. Johnson and Ms. Patel is key in this scenario since trust was previously built. Paraprofessionals work closely with some students and might develop a different perspective of these students' math strengths. However, they do not always have opportunities to share those perspectives with the classroom teacher. Teachers should work to build a relationship of trust with their paraprofessionals by asking for opinions and allowing for opportunities to reflect and critique.

Case 4.2 Problems with Small Groups

Positive relationships between teachers and families are essential, especially when issues arise in the classroom. This case demonstrates how Ms. Morales, a fifth-grade math teacher, incorporates group work and small group discussions as integral components of her math instruction. However, she receives an email from a student's parent describing participation concerns during math class, potentially connected to the student's hijab. The teacher and parent meet to discuss the reasons behind Ms. Morales's instructional decisions, and they also brainstorm ways to ensure the student feels safe, respected, and supported during small group time in math class. This class highlights the importance of classroom communities, considerations for grouping students, and the value of building partnerships with students' families.

We highlight the key points for consideration from the case as follows:

1. *Considerations When Grouping Students*

    There are many different purposes for grouping students. You might consider the content students are learning or how students get along with one another. However you decide to group students, it is important to change those groupings periodically. Ms. Morales changed the groups students were assigned to so that they had diverse perspectives when engaging in math discussions. Heterogeneous groupings (related to gender, race, ability, language, etc.) help students practice listening to and considering different ways of approaching and solving math problems. Questioning group members, justifying their thinking, critiquing the explanations, and cooperatively trying others' approaches allows students to develop a deeper, more connected understanding of math than if everyone in the group solved the problem in the same way.

2. *Building Safe Classroom Communities for Group Work*

Discussing rough draft math ideas might be scary for some students, particularly when an expectation has been set that the only math ideas worth discussing are those that are correct. Students may also engage in discussion differently depending on who is in their small group. In this case, Fatima became more reserved during group work once she started wearing her hijab. A hijab is an outward expression of a Muslim's identity, but misconceptions and negative stereotypes can lead Muslim students to feel unsafe or unwelcome in schools. Teachers can create an inclusive classroom community by having open and respectful conversations about different religions and cultures in their classrooms. This might mean that teachers will also need to educate themselves prior to having conversations with their students. However, make sure that if there are only a few students who identify from a particular cultural or religious background that they do not feel singled out during a discussion. In this context, dismantling misconceptions around the hijab will help female Muslim students make the transition to wearing the hijab with pride while they are in school. Classrooms where students feel supported and respected are ones where students are more likely to take risks by sharing their rough draft math ideas. Diversity in math ideas is essential for equitable math instruction

because it allows students to make connections and dig deeper into the math, which will improve math instruction for all students.
3. *Developing Positive Math Identities*

    Math identity is how students see themselves as learners and doers of math, and it is what math teachers should consider through all their instructional decisions. If Fatima continues to withdraw from math discussions, then she will start to internalize that her math ideas are not worth exploring or considering. For equitable math instruction to occur, teachers need to be aware of the students whose voices are not being heard and elevate those voices and ideas. This can be done by creating groupworthy tasks and setting up roles for group work where every student's contribution is essential to the success of the group. Ensuring all students play a pivotal role in small groups will help build positive math identities by showing them they are capable of doing math and, furthermore, they are important contributors in a group for learning math.

Case 4.3 Reframing and Valuing Student Voice

Students' contributions to math discussions are essential, and students need to know that their math ideas are valued and worth being considered by the class. This case illustrates how Ms. Cho, a first-grade teacher, leads a whole-group discussion on decomposing addends to benchmark ten as a strategy for addition. A focus on students' use of the word *decompose* in their explanations of their strategies brings to light questions about the importance of math vocabulary and valuing all forms of students' contributions.

We highlight the key points for consideration from the case as follows:

1. *Assuming Students' Identities*

    When you read this case, did you make an assumption about Bo's race? Ms. Cho's class is described as linguistically and racially diverse, but the students' identities are not stated on purpose. Would you interpret this case differently if you were told that Bo was an English learner from China or an English learner from Mexico? Would you interpret this case differently if Bo identified as a white American learner or a Black American learner? When a student uses informal language, assumptions might be made about who that student is and what that student is capable of doing in math class. If you interpret the case differently depending on Bo's race and language, then reflect on why you have differing expectations for different groups of students.

2. *Highlighting Students' Intellectual Contributions*

    Students' contributions to class discussions should be valued, especially when those contributions are publicly given. A teacher exhibits status in a class that guides how other students either value or devalue their peers' contributions. When Ms. Cho does not acknowledge Bo's contributions and instead asks Jamal to restate Bo's ideas, it makes Bo feel like his contribution was wrong. Publicly answering questions wrong in math class often makes students feel embarrassed and discourages them from sharing their ideas with the class. In this case, Bo showed physical signs of withdrawing from the class when he leaned back in his chair and avoided eye contact. Teachers need to create a classroom community that values and respects all forms of math contributions, especially ones that can continue to be revised and improved. Ms. Cho remedied the situation by publicly discussing the purpose of restating another's contribution to the discussion. Moving forward, she can also make sure to acknowledge Bo's contribution before asking another student to restate or build on Bo's ideas. This teacher move will highlight Bo's ideas as the class works collaboratively to refine the idea.

3. *Aligning Math Instruction with Math Goals*

    The goal of the lesson was to use a decomposing strategy to benchmark ten for addition. Bo provided a clear explanation of how he decomposed the number 5 to benchmark 10 when adding. Ms. Cho could have asked Bo additional questions to uncover how he decomposed the 5 pencils into 3 and 2 to make the addition easier. Instead, she chose to call on a student who would say the word *decompose* in his explanation. Ms. Cho's actions put a focus on using math vocabulary correctly instead of focusing on decomposing strategies to add quantities. Math vocabulary and attention to precision are important, but the math ideas behind students' contributions are the most important focus to discuss. All students, even those who might use informal language, should feel like they can and should share their strategies as an integral part of the whole-class math discussion. This will help to build positive math identities when their contributions are valued no matter if formal or informal math language is used.

Case 4.4 Math Is a Universal Language?

American teachers often attended school in America, which means many of their math experiences are similar. Without exposure to different ways of learning and using math, American teachers can be led to the incorrect belief that math is a universal language and is used in the same way across the world. American schools are made up of a beautiful diverse student population whose families come from all over the world. Their math experiences should be looked at as assets to be explored by everyone in the class, including their teachers.

This case shows Mr. Ronduen, a fourth-grade math teacher, teaching a place value unit at the beginning of the school year to a new group of students. In his class, he has a student who is new to the country, speaks limited English, and has learned a different way to write large numbers from her school in her home country. Through difficulties with communication between the teacher and this new student, this case explores issues related to power struggles, language practices in math class, and the assumptions that are made about math content.

We highlight the key points for consideration from the case as follows:

1. *Math Across the World*

   How quantities are represented and ways of calculating quantities are dependent on culture and societal norms. Ceyda is from Turkey, which follows the European notation of using a period to separate large quantities and a comma as a decimal separator. She has seen this notation in her home country and was taught this notation in Turkish schools. Mr. Ronduen learned the American notation for writing numbers and is only familiar with the American notation. The myth about math as a universal language is challenged here through the example of how numbers are written and read differently in different parts of the world.

   Beyond representations of numbers, there are also different standard algorithms that are used in math to calculate quantities. Though most countries use a base ten number system, there are still countries that do not. Without exposure to different representations and ways of doing math, teachers may fall to the incorrect belief about math as a universal language. Mr. Ronduen even states that "numbers are the same everywhere," which demonstrates his lack of exposure to math notations outside of the United States. It is important for teachers to get to know the background of their students and educate themselves on different math notations and strategies their students might use.

2. *Language Practices in Math Class*

   Mr. Ronduen was told by another teacher to create small groups of students who speak different home languages so that they have to speak English to one another. With the push for English as the official language, some schools may feel the best way for students to learn English is to only allow English to be spoken. However, students in math class are simultaneously learning the math content and English language, which requires more cognitive load than if they only had to learn math content. Students who are allowed to use their home language in math class can significantly enhance their understanding of math concepts by putting the focus on the math. Through discussions with students who speak a similar language, English learners can improve their communication about math and practice how to communicate their math understanding in English.

Dictionaries are often thought to be an appropriate tool for multilingual students, but remember that this tool requires a level of home language proficiency to use it accurately. Not all students, especially in elementary school, will come with the needed language proficiency or knowledge of how to use dictionaries. Luckily, Ceyda did have previous experience with a translation dictionary and was able to use it to help with the math task. In addition to dictionaries, math teachers can use pictures and manipulatives to help students understand new content and provide a way for students to communicate their math thinking.

3. *Power Struggles*

Teachers are in a position of power over students. Teachers make the rules, assign grades, and ultimately decide the academic fate of their students. In this case, Ceyda completed the math task by writing the standard form of numbers with the period as the separator, which is what she learned in Turkey. Ceyda demonstrated her power when she wrote what she learned to be the correct notations and shared that work with her small group, even though it was different from the rest of the class.

Once Mr. Ronduen joined Ceyda's small group, the power dynamics shifted so that Mr. Ronduen had the power. He publicly told her that her work was wrong and then wrote on her paper. This public display of his power had an impact on the students in the class. First, it communicated to Ceyda that her math ideas are not valid. Second, it communicates to the class that the teacher is the only one with the correct way of thinking, which reinforces the teacher's power.

In this case, we see that Ceyda begins to shut down as she processes what just happened. The power struggle will impact Ceyda's math identity in her new school and her sense of safety in class. She might begin to question if math makes sense or if she should continue trying. The power struggle between Mr. Ronduen and Ceyda also has implications for other students who witnessed what happened. Molli tried to make sense of Ceyda's work and even commented that maybe Ceyda was taught differently. Mr. Ronduen's dismissal of Molli's idea will guide students to make incorrect assumptions about Ceyda's math understanding.

Case 4.5 Building Math Confidence Through Asset-Based Language

In many classrooms, math instruction can unintentionally send the message that being "right" is more important than being thoughtful, curious, or willing to try. This case highlights how teachers can use asset-based language and inclusive communication to shift that narrative. When a kindergarten student, Jay, confidently shares an incorrect combination of Unifix cubes to make ten, Mr. Guyton responds with encouragement rather than correction, using the moment as an opportunity for collective problem-solving and peer support. By doing so, the teacher normalizes checking peers' work as part of learning, encourages students to revise their thinking, and reinforces the idea that everyone has something valuable to contribute. Mr. Guyton uses his role as a teacher to do more than deliver content, for he establishes classroom norms that position all students as capable mathematicians. He considers ways for students to build on each other's ideas through peer dialogue, gestures, and manipulatives.

The case invites reflection on how our language, expectations, and norms shape students' math identities. When classrooms are built on mutual respect, trust, and affirmation, students begin to see themselves and their peers as capable mathematicians. These moments aren't just about content; they're about cultivating confidence, fostering agency, and creating a space where students feel safe to explore ideas in all stages of formation. Teachers across all grade levels can find inspiration in these practices and consider how small shifts in language and classroom culture can make a big difference in students' willingness to engage, take risks, and grow as math thinkers.

We highlight the key points for consideration from the case as follows:

1. *Asset-Based Language Builds Student Confidence and Identity*
   Throughout the lesson, Mr. Guyton uses language that positions students as capable and thoughtful mathematicians. He refers to Jay's thinking as "brilliant" and affirms Charles's observation by saying, "Wonderful, Charles." These moments illustrate how intentional, affirming language communicates that students' ideas are valuable, even when they are still forming. By thanking students for their contributions and providing nonverbal affirmations like "raised claps" and "air high fives," Mr. Guyton validates participation and builds students' confidence in student-friendly ways. The case challenges teachers to examine whether their classroom talk uplifts student voices, particularly for those who may lack confidence in math or struggle to express themselves fluently. Affirming identities through language is a powerful way to build long-term confidence and engagement.
2. *Mistakes Are Opportunities for Learning and Belonging*
   Mr. Guyton's classroom culture reframes mistakes as essential parts of learning rather than failures. When Jay incorrectly combines 6 red cubes and 5 blue cubes to make 10, Mr. Guyton doesn't correct him. Instead, he responds with warmth and gratitude: "Thank you for sharing your thinking, Jay!" and invites the class to

investigate together. This approach shifts the focus from right or wrong answers to the thinking process itself. Students like Vera and Charles engage respectfully, helping Jay revise his solution without embarrassment. This kind of learning community shows how errors can build math understanding while also reinforcing social belonging. It's important for teachers to reflect on how their own classrooms send the message that mistakes are expected, welcomed, and even celebrated as part of the math journey.

3. *Classroom Norms Shape Student Discourse and Peer Support*

    A defining feature of Mr. Guyton's classroom is the establishment of clear, collaborative norms. Students are expected to listen to one another, revise their thinking, and offer help in kind and respectful ways. These norms are not just teacher-directed—they are reinforced by the students themselves. Charles summarizes Jay's learning process without judgment, saying, "Jay said 6 and 5. He counted again and said 6 and 4. It's OK to count again." Such student-to-student interactions are evidence that the classroom environment invites productive struggle and encourages supportive dialogue. These norms help all students to contribute through gestures, manipulatives, and conversation. Teachers are encouraged to reflect on how they introduce and revisit norms that position students as collaborators and co-constructors of knowledge.

4. *Affirming Classrooms Require Intentional Leadership and Shared Practice*

    In this case, the role of school leadership is recognized in providing feedback for and scaling equity-focused instructional practices. Dr. Thompson, the administrator, notices the inclusive culture of Mr. Guyton's classroom and encourages him to share his approach with colleagues through professional learning. This shows how affirming math spaces are a result of intentional planning, reflection, and leadership. The case prompts teachers and schools to deepen equitable math practices and create structures, such as peer observation, collaborative planning, and shared reflection, that can support initiatives targeting asset-based communication. Teachers and leaders alike must ask: How can we create opportunities for teachers to learn from one another and sustain environments where all students feel seen, heard, and capable in math?

CHAPTER 5 POINTS FOR CONSIDERATION

Cases About Math Instructional Pedagogies and Tasks

Case 5.1 Gender and Binary Story Problems

Many elementary teachers strive to create meaningful, engaging math lessons by using real-life contexts that are relevant to their students. However, even well-intentioned instructional choices can inadvertently create moments of exclusion when they are not responsive to the diverse identities present in the classroom. In this case, a familiar part-part-whole story problem framed around binary gender categories leads to an uncomfortable moment for a first-grade student who identifies outside the gender binary. As students debate whether this classmate "counts" as a boy or a girl, the unintended impact of the language used in the problem becomes clear. This scenario reflects a common challenge many teachers face: how to design math tasks that reflect and respect the lived experiences of *all* students while still meeting instructional goals.

Ms. Glen, an experienced first-grade teacher, realizes the need to move beyond pre-planned lessons and toward more flexible, inclusive approaches to teaching math. Her story serves as a powerful reminder of the importance of anticipating how pedagogical instruction, even with everyday math problems, can shape students' sense of identity and belonging. The case encourages teachers to examine the assumptions embedded in their instructional materials, particularly around gender, and to seek ways to adapt problems to be more affirming and inclusive. It also highlights the value of responsive teaching and the need to listen, reflect, and make adjustments, an essential practice for both advancing equity and supporting rich math thinking. Ultimately, even small shifts in language and lesson design can create more welcoming spaces where all students feel seen, respected, and safe to engage in learning.

We highlight the key points for consideration from the case as follows:

1. *Planning Contextual Story Problems*

    Part-part-whole relationships involve combining two parts to create one whole, which connects to the idea that numbers are embedded in other numbers. First-grade students solve word problems that involve part-part-whole relationships where one of the parts is unknown. This can be challenging for some students because part-part-whole relationships do not contain an action for the students to act out, but instead, students have to generalize what the objects have in common to determine the whole, two parts, and then calculate the unknown part.

    Contextualizing these part-part-whole relationships into objects or concepts the students are familiar with will help them to understand the relationships so they can focus on calculating. However, it is important to remember that every student in the class might not have the same background information or prior experiences.

    In the story, the teacher used a story problem that had represented her previous classes but did not represent the students in her current class. It caused confusion for the class and created a classroom environment that was not safe for Sam. It is essential for teachers to keep their current students in mind as they plan lessons, particularly when they are deciding how to contextualize story problems. Modifying lessons to meet the needs of students does take additional time, but it is an important aspect of equitable math teaching.

2. *Focusing on Students and Their Math Thinking*

    Focusing on students' math thinking involves more than just listening to correct answers, for it means learning about students as whole people and valuing the diverse perspectives they bring to math. In this case, Sam's identity was unintentionally disregarded, which disrupted both their math engagement and sense of safety. To truly center students, teachers can take time to learn about students' experiences, interests, and identities, and consider how those elements show up in their math thinking and participation. Questions like "Whose voices are being centered?" and "Who might feel left out or misrepresented by this task?" can guide planning and reflection. Teachers can also provide open-ended tasks that allow for multiple approaches and invite students to explain their reasoning, ensuring each student feels their thinking is valued and seen.

3. *Intentionally Use Identity-Affirming Language and Representations*

    The language used in math tasks plays a key role in shaping students' sense of belonging in math class. Teachers should strive to use inclusive, identity-affirming language that respects students' diverse backgrounds and avoids reinforcing stereotypes or binary categories that do not exist. In math story problems, this might mean choosing neutral or varied names, reflecting different family dynamics, and avoiding gendered groupings. For example, instead of asking, "How many students are boys and girls?" a more inclusive version might be, "How many students are wearing green or another color?" Encouraging students to create or adapt story problems based on their own experiences can also foster greater inclusion and agency. A simple rule of thumb to consider is as follows: If a context could misrepresent or marginalize someone, there's likely a more affirming alternative.

4. *Creating Inclusive and Responsive Instructional Strategies and Routines*

    Recognizing equitable instructional strategies and routines is essential for promoting equity and ensuring all students can fully participate in math learning. In the case of the gender-based story problem, the assumption that gender categorization would be a neutral strategy led to unintended harm, highlighting the need to regularly examine and adjust participation structures. Teachers can foster inclusion by designing flexible tasks that allow for self-identification or use of interests to form groups, rather than relying on predefined categories. To make the tasks more meaningful, teachers can collaborate with students to co-create participation expectations, giving them ownership over how they engage in the classroom.

Teachers should also take time to critically reflect on their lesson planning routines to ensure they are responsive to the diverse identities of their current students. While efficient lesson planning is valuable, true equity requires intentional adjustments that align with students' needs, experiences, and identities. This reflection encourages teachers to ask important questions like, "Whose perspectives are represented in our math problems?" and "How can we make sure all students see themselves reflected in the classroom?" Adapting lessons doesn't mean starting from scratch each day; rather, it means being willing to make thoughtful changes based on student input or collaboration with colleagues. Even small changes, such as revising story problems or adjusting how students participate, can create a more inclusive and equitable classroom environment. Ultimately, this approach fosters a culture of care and responsiveness, where students feel valued, supported, and empowered in their math learning.

Case 5.2 Using Technology to Practice Place Value

Sra. Garcia, a second-grade teacher in a predominantly Latinx school, introduced Dash robots into her math lessons to enhance students' understanding of place value. The activity, which required students to program the robots to demonstrate the expanded form of a three-digit number, aimed to engage students through hands-on learning with technology. However, the lesson revealed an equity issue: Students with more experience using technology at home, like Ana and Rafael, quickly took on leadership roles and dominated the task, while students with limited access to technology, like Maria and Nicolás, faced more challenges to engage. This imbalance led to passive participation from some students and highlighted the importance of ensuring that all students have equal access to the skills and tools needed to fully engage in technology-driven learning experiences.

This case raises important considerations for teachers when integrating technology into math instruction, especially in diverse classrooms with varying levels of access to resources. While tools like Dash robots can enhance engagement and learning, it's crucial for teachers to recognize the disparities in technological proficiency and provide foundational support to ensure all students can participate meaningfully. Sra. Garcia's experience serves as a reminder that in order for technology to truly enhance learning, teachers must be mindful of access issues and design activities that promote shared participation. Offering differentiated instruction and questioning the equity of lesson structures can help ensure that all students, regardless of their technological background, are given the opportunity to participate in learning math.

We highlight the key points for consideration from the case as follows:

1. *Understanding Place Value Through Technology and Multiple Representations*

    Using technology, such as Dash robots, provides students with a dynamic way to explore place value concepts. By engaging in an activity where they physically move the robot across a floor grid to represent hundreds, tens, and ones, students can visualize and manipulate place values in a concrete way. This method not only reinforces the abstract concept of place value but also encourages critical thinking as students plan and program the robot's movements. To maximize learning, teachers can incorporate additional visual aids, like floor grids or number charts, to further anchor the abstract concept of place value in a tactile and interactive environment. Encouraging students to explain their reasoning as they code and manipulate the robot ensures they understand the underlying math concepts, as well as how the technology supports their learning.

Moreover, the integration of technology into math instruction serves as an excellent opportunity to reinforce both math skills and problem-solving abilities. As students use the Blockly programming language to direct the robot, they are engaged in critical thinking as they break down numbers and identify their place values. Teachers can enhance the lesson by incorporating open-ended questions that prompt students to reflect on the connections between math and technology. For example, asking students to explain why the robot's movements match the expanded form of the number deepens their understanding of both place value and the role of technology in their learning. Teachers can also create opportunities for students to take on different roles in coding, programming, and explaining the robot's path, which would help develop their understanding of place value concepts.

2. *Access and Agency*

The case highlights disparities in students' access to technology and how it can influence their agency within the classroom. Ana and Rafael, who have more access to technology at home, quickly take control of the task when compared to Maria and Nicolás, who have limited experience with technology at home. This creates an imbalance, limiting the ability of all students to fully participate and assert their agency. Teachers must be aware of how unequal access to resources can impact student engagement and ensure that all students are equipped with the skills necessary to use technology effectively.

3. *Inclusive and Response Teaching Practices*

Sra. Garcia's assumption that all students would be able to adapt to using Dash robots based on their general experience with technology at home highlights an important oversight in recognizing individual student needs. To foster a more inclusive learning environment, it is essential for teachers to differentiate instruction based on varying levels of technological proficiency. For students with limited access to technology, providing additional foundational support ensures that everyone has the opportunity to engage meaningfully with the lesson. Offering differentiated levels of support, whether through peer collaboration or hands-on guidance, helps to ensure that all students have an equitable chance to participate and succeed in technology-enhanced lessons.

Furthermore, this case illuminates the need for culturally and contextually responsive teaching, especially in classrooms with diverse student backgrounds, such as Sra. Garcia's class, where students come from a range of socioeconomic contexts. When integrating technology, teachers must be mindful of these differences and design lessons that account for the unique needs of their students. Acknowledging the cultural and socioeconomic factors that influence student experiences with technology enables teachers to create a more equitable environment. By fostering inclusive practices that ensure all students, regardless of their home background, have access to the tools and opportunities needed to succeed, teachers can promote both engagement and learning in a way that supports every student's growth and development.

4. *Power Dynamics in Group Work*

The inequitable distribution of roles in the group work activity, where certain students dominate while others are relegated to passive roles, addresses the importance of considering how power dynamics are shaped within group tasks. To avoid reinforcing existing inequalities, teachers should establish clear, equitable expectations for participation and consider ways to rotate roles and responsibilities, so all students have an opportunity to take on leadership and collaborative roles. Ensuring that all students are actively involved can prevent marginalization and help foster a more inclusive learning environment.

Case 5.3 Overcoming Roadblocks in a "Race to Mastery"

Many teachers introduce classroom structures and routines with the best intentions—motivating students, tracking progress, and celebrating milestones. But what happens when those same systems unintentionally undermine student confidence, reinforce stereotypes, or perpetuate speed and correct solutions as being proficient in math? In this case, a third-grade teacher named Ms. Applegate realizes that her well-meaning timed multiplication tests and public race track display are causing some students, like Emma, to feel anxious and believe damaging gender-based assumptions about who is "good at math." Despite Emma's strength in using real-world problem-solving skills rooted in her family's farming work, she begins to internalize the idea that she can't succeed in math because she isn't fast or male.

This case highlights the importance of critically examining instructional practices and the messages they send to students about ability, identity, and belonging. As Ms. Applegate reflects on her classroom norms and explores more equitable strategies, she shifts from emphasizing speed to honoring flexibility and real-life connections. By centering students' lived experiences and recognizing their cultural and community assets, she helps Emma, and other students, reclaim their confidence as capable math learners. Teachers reading this story are invited to consider how seemingly neutral practices may carry unintended consequences and how a responsive shift in approach can create more inclusive and empowering learning environments.

We highlight the key points for consideration from the case as follows:

1. *Flexibility in Math Fluency Matters*

    Timed tests often emphasize speed, which can misrepresent what it means to be mathematically fluent. In this case, Ms. Applegate realized that fluency involves more than rapid recall—it includes understanding, strategic thinking, and flexibility. Thus, she begins to question the timed tests and what they may be miscommunicating about what math is and who is "good at math."

By encouraging Emma to think about multiplication through real-life scenarios, such as feeding animals on her farm, Ms. Applegate supported a more comprehensive and accurate understanding of fluency that values diverse problem-solving strategies connected to applied skills.

2. *Promoting Student Agency and Confidence*

When Emma compared herself to faster peers and concluded she wasn't "good at math," it became clear that classroom structures were affecting her sense of agency. Shifting away from competitive assessments can allow students to share their own strategies and see themselves as capable math thinkers. Like in this case, Emma was able to use her agricultural background to connect with the math content, making it more accessible and personally meaningful. This empowered Emma to recognize the math she already does and reposition herself as mathematically competent.

3. *Challenging Gender Stereotypes*

When Emma expressed that "boys are better at math," it became clear that the competitive structure of the timed tests and race track display had contributed to the formation of gendered assumptions about ability. These unintended consequences show how classroom norms, especially those that publicly rank students, can send implicit messages about who belongs in math and who is expected to excel. Ms. Applegate's willingness to pause, reflect, and pivot her approach is a powerful reminder that effective teaching involves more than delivering content—it requires ongoing attention to the messages our methods communicate. By shifting her practice to affirm Emma's strengths and value multiple ways of engaging with math, Ms. Applegate helped disrupt gendered narratives and create a more inclusive environment where all students could see themselves as capable mathematicians.

4. *Affirming Math Thinking*

Ms. Applegate shifted away from valuing only speed-based performance, recognizing the importance of students' own ways of reasoning and problem-solving. She encouraged Emma to use feed ratios and grouping strategies that were relevant for her, thereby affirming such strategies and examples as valid math thinking. Additionally, Ms. Applegate redefined what it means to participate in math learning by removing the public comparison tool and creating spaces for individual student contributions. By reimagining participation, all students' ways of thinking were honored, and new norms were established that positioned students as "doers of math."

This case exemplifies the idea that not all students "pop" at the same pace in math. Some students may develop speed or strategies earlier, while others, like Emma, need time and different contexts to reveal their math strengths. Just as every popcorn kernel has its own timing and heat conditions to pop, every student deserves the space to flourish without being judged by others' timelines or performance norms. Equitable math instruction requires valuing all contributions, whether they emerge quickly or slowly, and recognizing that brilliance comes in many forms.

Case 5.4 Comparing Fractions in Safe Spaces with Number Talks

This case addresses the powerful intersection of instructional practices and the creation of inclusive, equitable learning environments. Many educators strive to foster classrooms where every student feels seen, heard, and valued, particularly during moments of academic discourse like number talks. Yet, those efforts can be complicated by underlying social dynamics, including cultural and linguistic differences, power imbalances among peers, and harmful stereotypes. Teachers often navigate these challenges while simultaneously introducing new instructional strategies, making it all the more critical to attend intentionally to classroom norms and the lived experiences students bring with them.

In this case, we see the importance of addressing racism directly and using instructional moments to affirm students' math thinking, especially for those whose voices are often marginalized. By intentionally highlighting Adrian's contribution and guiding the class to unpack his reasoning, Ms. Lee not only disrupted deficit narratives but also modeled how meaningful participation in math can look different for each student. Teachers who aim to cultivate safe, student-centered classrooms can find resonance in this example, recognizing the need to pair strong pedagogical routines with culturally responsive and affirming practices that support all learners.

We highlight the key points for consideration from the case as follows:

1. *Reinforcing Number Sense and Diverse Students' Strategies*

    Did you learn an algorithm for comparing two fractions, such as cross-multiplication? Too often procedures are used to compare fractions with no thought about the size of the fractions, which only reinforces the idea that math is about following rules. Equitable math teaching requires students to build a conceptual understanding that connects to their prior knowledge, which in turn builds number sense. Adrian's approach to comparing fractions, called closeness to a benchmark, demonstrated his number sense of decomposing fractional amounts ($\frac{5}{8} = \frac{4}{8} + \frac{1}{8}$), identify equivalent fractions ($\frac{4}{8} = \frac{5}{10}$), and comparing unit fractions ($\frac{1}{8} > \frac{1}{10}$). Adrian efficiently used his strategy to compare the fractions and demonstrated a much deeper understanding than someone who simply uses the cross-multiplication procedure.

    When Ms. Lee chose to highlight Adrian's thinking and unpack it with the class, she affirmed the validity of his math thinking. This moment helped challenge dominant norms about who is perceived as mathematically capable and the value in learning from others to appreciate new perspectives. Teachers can foster this kind of inclusive math environment by encouraging multiple strategies, validating student reasoning, and guiding the class to explore and make sense of different methods together. Purposefully seeking out and lifting up strategies from students whose voices may be marginalized can empower those students and broaden all learners' views of what counts as *doing math*.

2. *Creating Norms for Respectful Discourse Using Instructional Routines*

    For instructional routines like number talks to truly support equitable learning, teachers must intentionally create classroom environments where all students feel safe, respected, and encouraged to share their ideas. While number talks have the potential to promote meaningful math discourse and shift the focus from teacher-led instruction to student thinking, these benefits can only be realized when supported by strong norms around respectful interactions and inclusivity. Ms. Lee's approach demonstrated how thoughtful facilitation and responsiveness to her instruction, such as giving students wait time, using nonverbal signals, and validating multiple strategies, can support participation from all learners. At the same time, she had to remain vigilant about the emotional and social safety of students, particularly in the face of harmful peer interactions. Teachers can co-develop norms with students that explicitly name expectations for listening, disagreeing respectfully, and supporting one another. By embedding equity into discourse structures, teachers not only promote deeper math understanding but also foster a sense of belonging and shared responsibility for each other's success.

3. *Teachers Must Actively Interrupt Bias While Elevating Marginalized Voices*

    The case clearly demonstrates how racism can show up in subtle and overt ways, impacting students' sense of safety and willingness to participate. Ms. Lee's decision to focus on Adrian's math reasoning was one form of intervention, for she elevated Adrian's status and positioned him to be accepted by his peers. However, ongoing efforts are needed to explicitly address bias and build a classroom community that rejects discrimination. Teachers can prepare themselves to recognize and respond to harmful behaviors, cultivate allyship among students (as seen in Brett's supportive response), and consistently center the strengths and contributions of multilingual and immigrant students. Equity in math is not only about access to content but also about creating spaces where all students' identities and ways of knowing are respected and celebrated.

Case 5.5 Stuck in the Script

In many classrooms, teachers face the challenge of delivering math instruction using scripted or prepackaged curricula that may not reflect the lived experiences of their students. This case explores the tension between following a curriculum with fidelity and adapting lessons to be more culturally and contextually relevant to students' experiences and learning needs. In this case, a word problem about sharing carnival tickets created confusion and disengagement—not because the math was too difficult but because the context was unfamiliar. Students spent more time trying to make sense of the scenario than solving the math problem, revealing how even well-intended lessons can miss the mark when they do not connect with students' backgrounds.

This case encourages teachers to reflect on how lesson contexts impact student access to math content. It raises important questions: When does sticking to the script become a barrier to equity? How can teachers preserve the math goals of a lesson while modifying the context to make it more meaningful and engaging for their students? Should teachers use the unfamiliar context to broaden students' experiences? The case invites teachers to consider how they might use their professional judgment to adapt curriculum in ways that do not stray from the math learning goals but rather provide more opportunity for student understanding and confidence.

We highlight the key points for consideration from the case as follows:

1. *Context Matters*

    This case illuminates how the cultural and experiential context embedded in a math problem can influence student engagement and access. When word problems reflect settings, experiences, or values unfamiliar to students, they risk becoming barriers to learning rather than conduits for understanding. For Ms. Daniels' students, the scripted scenario of a carnival and ride tickets proved to be distant from their realities, which distracted them from focusing on the math goal of equal sharing and remainders. Several students questioned what a carnival was or shared different cultural interpretations, highlighting how assumptions embedded in problems can unintentionally exclude or confuse learners. When problems are situated in familiar activities like sharing snacks at a classroom party, students can focus their cognitive energy on the math itself rather than decoding an unfamiliar scenario.

    To design tasks that leverage contextual relevance, teachers must ask, "Do my students have the background knowledge and cultural frame of reference to connect with this task?" Answering this question requires teachers to invest time in getting to know their students, which, in turn, guides intentional decisions about when and how to adapt instructional materials to ensure relevance and accessibility. This is exactly the kind of reflective practice Ms. Daniels demonstrated after her lesson, as she considered how to reframe the problem in a way that would feel meaningful and approachable to her students. A different approach Ms. Daniels could take would be to not use the unfamiliar context as an opportunity to broaden students' experiences of carnivals by making connections to their cultural interpretations. No change would need to be made to the scripted curriculum, and students could have the opportunity to learn about new contexts.

2. *Fidelity of Math Content in Scripted Curricula*
   The case also raises concerns about the fidelity of math content in scripted curricula. When we define fidelity too narrowly, we risk valuing surface-level compliance over deep, meaningful learning. But honoring the integrity of a lesson doesn't mean giving up our professional judgment. In fact, it calls on us to use it. Ms. Daniels' decision to consider swapping the unfamiliar carnival scenario with something her students could relate to, like sharing snacks at a class party, isn't stepping away from the curriculum; it's stepping toward her students. However, it is important for Ms. Daniels to have a strong understanding of the intended math goals to ensure that adapting a lesson keeps those math goals intact. While the context can be made more accessible, relevant, and engaging, the amount of math thinking that is required to meet the lesson's goal should be maintained.
3. *Advocating for Teacher Agency and Student Access*
   The case illustrates the ongoing tension many teachers feel between following a mandated, scripted curriculum and doing what they know is best for their students. Advocating for teacher agency isn't about resisting expectations—it's about ensuring that curriculum serves students, not the other way around. When teachers are trusted to adapt materials thoughtfully, they can create space for more equitable and engaging instruction. To support this, teachers might begin by asking themselves reflective questions like: What data (e.g., student work, questions, behavior) suggests students are or aren't accessing the task as intended? And, what small adaptations could make a big difference in how students engage with this content?
   In addition to internal reflection, building agency also involves seeking support and starting conversations. Teachers can bring examples of successful adaptations to grade-level meetings and professional learning communities, inviting colleagues to share and reflect together. They can approach instructional coaches or administrators

with evidence that shows how their adjustments support student learning without compromising standards. By taking these steps, teachers can advocate not only for themselves but for their students, ensuring every child sees their world reflected in the math they learn.

CHAPTER 6 POINTS FOR CONSIDERATION

Cases About Engaging Families and Communities in Math

Case 6.1 Supporting Multilingual Families with Math Content

Mr. Green, a fifth-grade math teacher, understands that partnerships with families are important for his students' success with the challenging math content he will teach. As an English-speaking teacher, Mr. Green has little knowledge of languages to help him communicate with his students' families. An open house event demonstrates the language support Mr. Green used to try to bridge the communication gap with families to discuss expectations and concerns for the upcoming school year. This case highlights the importance of building inclusive communication with families, technology use for communicating math goals, and considerations for whose math strategies should be explored in school.

We highlight the key points for consideration from the case as follows:

1. *Inclusive Communication with Families*

    All students' families should be given the opportunity to be knowledgeable about their child's education. Mr. Green found ways to communicate with families who did not speak English by providing time for translation between students and their adults during the open house. He also created a presentation that included minimal use of words and instead used pictures to visually communicate his expectations for the upcoming year. When a parent asked for support with helping her child with math homework, Mr. Green suggested that he would make short video explanations using software that would allow families to pick captions in their home language.

Beyond language considerations, not all families could attend the open house. It should not be assumed that families who do not attend school functions somehow care less about their children than the families who do attend. The school function could conflict with a work schedule, there could be a prior commitment for the family, there could be transportation concerns, and many other reasons teachers should consider. Mr. Green understood this, and instead of judging the families, he recorded the open house presentation to post the video to the class website. This intentional act of inclusion allowed families who could not attend the open house to be informed about their children's education.

2. *Communicating Math Goals*

Recent math strategies taught in schools tend to focus on students' building a conceptual understanding of math rather than just a procedural understanding. Because of this, families might not be familiar with the math strategies students are learning or the reasoning behind why math is taught in a particular way. As math teachers, communicating *why* certain strategies are learned in school is just as important as demonstrating how those strategies work.

Ms. Qutob expresses how the math is different from what she knows, and she does not know how to help her son. Ms. Udalor agreed and even said that it has made homework time frustrating. From the concerns of these parents, it sounds like the families' math strategies are not valued in the same way as the math strategies taught in schools. Since math strategies can vary across countries, it would be advantageous for Mr. Green to take the time and learn about the math strategies that the parents are knowledgeable about. Recognizing and drawing from students' families as resources for learning math can affirm students' math identities and promote their math learning.

3. *Translation Using Technology*

Teachers have access to an ever-changing landscape of technology tools that can increase communication with families. Ms. Udalor asked if Mr. Green's videos could be created in a way where families could pick captions in their own language. AI can generate subtitles for videos, provide a translated transcript of videos, and even use voice cloning to translate videos into families' home languages. There are also tools for translating documents into different languages. Teachers often need to consider the cost of such services, and there are many free options that can be found online. These free translation services can be helpful for providing support for families.

Case 6.2 Advocating Access to Extracurricular Math Activities

Math enrichment programs should be inclusive of all students who might be interested in participating. This case illustrates how Ms. Ramirez, a fourth-grade math teacher, advocated for inclusivity during a Math Family Night event. One of the organizations that attended the event used recruitment materials that did not represent the students at the school, and the enrichment programs were unattainable for most families due to price and transportation to an outside location. This case highlights the importance of advocating for students and challenging the biases others may have.

We highlight the key points for consideration from the case as follows:

1. *Access to Math Enrichment*

    Extracurricular activities, like the after-school and summer programs offered through SparkMath, can provide opportunities for students to go deeper with math content and explore interests outside of what is taught in math class. When SparkMath decided to host a table at the Math Family Night of Lakewood Elementary, the organization should have researched the demographics of the students at the school. Children are more likely to want to participate in activities that they feel are connected to their identity in some way. When SparkMath targeted their recruitment materials based on who they assumed would be customers, their bias alienated groups of students and families and made them feel like SparkMath was not meant for them.

Additional barriers to accessing SparkMath enrichment include the language of the promotion materials, the cost of after-school math investigations and summer enrichment programs, and the off-school location of these programs. When families cannot read the promotional materials, and if no one at the table speaks their home language, then families may choose to skip the table and miss out on a potentially good opportunity for their child. The cost for this program could also be a hindrance for families who are working to provide housing, food, and clothing for their children. In low-income areas, like where Lakewood Elementary is located, discounted rates or scholarships could ensure that money is not the reason for limited access to math enrichment. The location of SparkMath is also an access issue for families who rely on the bus system to take students to and from school. Many programs will often move their activities to the school site to ensure easy access for students, which is what SparkMath did in the end.

2. *Advocating for Students Beyond the Math Classroom*

As teachers, we know you all care deeply for students and become invested in their lives beyond the classroom. However, you might feel that you have no control over what happens to your students once they leave the protection of your class. The first step to advocating for your students is to get to know them and their families. Listen to their stories and learn their needs. Then consider the systems, policies, and processes at the school that impact your students and do not meet their needs. Ms. Ramirez had to know the needs of her students and their families to recognize that SparkMath was not inclusive in its offerings. She then had to speak up to the director of SparkMath to educate him on why his marketing tactics and offerings were biased. Luckily, Mr. Williams was receptive to Ms. Ramirez and decided to make changes with his organization. When you choose to advocate for your students, the outcome might not initially be the same, but it should not stop you from speaking up for what you know to be right for your students.

Case 6.3 Navigating Family Help with Homework

Math learning happens beyond the classroom, and communication with families is essential for helping students build a conceptual understanding of math. This case shows how Ms. Goyal, a second-grade teacher, focuses her math lesson and homework on building a conceptual understanding of regrouping by using base ten blocks. Through a class discussion of students' strategies, the second-grade students practiced regrouping using base ten blocks when subtracting two-digit numbers and took home manipulatives to continue practicing for homework. Mr. Goyal has to reflect on how to communicate her instructional decisions with her students' families while also respecting the math knowledge they share with the children.

We highlight the key points for consideration from the case as follows:

1. *Many Valid Math Strategies*

    Due to limited exposure to multiple methods for calculating numbers, there can be the belief that there is one "right way" to subtract numbers. This was demonstrated through the note from Maneesh's mom. Algorithms, or the step-by-step process for calculating, can vary between cultures and countries. Some of these algorithms make the math process of calculating more explicit, or the algorithms hide the math understanding behind the process. Some algorithms might be faster or more efficient with some numbers, and other algorithms might be more efficient with a different set of numbers. No matter the case, an algorithm in itself is no more valid than another algorithm. Students should always be able to explain why their math strategies work as they move through the developmental process of making connections between physical representations to abstract representations of calculating quantities. Once students understand how different strategies work for calculating numbers, they can then pick the strategy that they feel is best for the numbers they need to calculate.

2. *Communicating Your Math Message to Families*

    Adults who are not teachers can often forget what it was like to learn some math concepts for the first time. There might also be the assumption that their own personal math experiences are how their child will learn best. As teachers, we rely on research on how children learn to make sense of math. Then we get to see that research in practice as children grapple with math content in different ways. This unique perspective on children learning math for the first time is something that should be shared with family members. Ms. Goyal could send communication home describing how using base ten blocks will help students visualize the regrouping that will later be shown using a standard algorithm. She could also begin the school year by communicating helpful ways families could support their children with homework. Setting these expectations at the beginning of the school year could limit families from completing homework for their child, which is what is shown in this case. Ms. Goyal could also map out the progression of the lessons for each unit and the reasoning behind the progression to help families understand instructional decisions that are made.

3. *Valuing the Math Knowledge of Families*

    Ms. Goyal's response to the note from Maneesh's mom is critical for Maneesh and the other students who witnessed the interactions. Though Ms. Goyal was upset by the note, she did not show this emotion to Maneesh nor take it out on him. Instead, Ms. Goyal asked Maneesh questions about what he was confused about and even positioned Maneesh as having the math understanding needed to explain the regrouping strategies to his mom.

Other students joined the conversation by stating how their own families reacted to the homework. Ms. Goyal knows that she should not put children in the middle of a disagreement between her and their families, so she dropped the conversation and walked away. Instead, she could have had Maneesh share his new strategy and have the class explore how that strategy works using the base ten blocks. This connection would value the math knowledge of Maneesh's family while also making a direct connection to what was learned in class.

Case 6.4 Exploring Community Partnerships to Enhance Math Applications

Math can be used to empower people to identify and solve real-world problems within their communities. This case provides an example of how Ms. Carter, a third-grade teacher, collaborated with a community member to create a community garden math project for her students to practice area and perimeter. The third-grade students became so excited by the project that they asked the community member if they could help build the gardens that were designed. This case highlights the importance of drawing from community knowledge, using math to enact social change, and empowering young children to make a difference in their community.

We highlight the key points for consideration from the case as follows:

1. *Real-Life Applications of Math Content*

    It is important that students see the value in what they learn in math class and recognize the applications of the content in real life. Students will become more engaged when learning math content when they have to use it to solve a real-life problem. Students who might not typically be engaged during math lessons could find the practical application more meaningful and build a deeper connection with the math concepts. In this case, the third-graders learned about the local Indigenous community and how they used math concepts to build sustainable spaces. Students became excited and wanted to contribute to the community garden that shares food with the local community. Ms. Carter's math lesson empowered her students to use math to support their community.

Area and perimeter are measurement topics that students often get confused with one another. Using real-life applications of area and perimeter can help students make connections to this content beyond memorizing vocabulary words and applying formulas. Also, the project allowed students to design the garden bed in different ways to fit within a space and then calculate the needed materials. The project demonstrates to students how real-life math could allow for multiple solutions and is more complex than just answering questions on a worksheet. The project could also be extended by having students determine different areas for the types of plants that are grown to maximize food for the community.

2. *Reaching Out to Community Members*

Schools bring value to the community because they teach children how to be productive and caring members of the community. Part of being caring members of a community is becoming familiar with its members and their needs. Ms. Carter exposed her students to Lily's grandfather, Mr. Redbird, so they could learn about the Indigenous members of their community. This exposure helps students see similarities between their own families and Indigenous families, which sparked students' interest in supporting their community members by helping create more community gardens. Reaching out to community members might seem daunting the first time, but many members of a community want to feel involved and valued in the development of the next generation.

Case 6.5 Flea Market Experience

Our identities are often not static and can vary depending on the situation. Our behaviors and how we perceive ourselves depend on the context we are in. Children may be more comfortable with their families or friends, and their identity might be more confident or playful in those contexts rather than when they are in school. This is why getting to know your students beyond the classroom is essential for understanding their full identities. Many schools encourage teachers to learn about their students by engaging with them and their families outside of school. This scenario reflects two teachers who went to see their students outside of school.

Macella and Nina each have one of the Reyes twins in their kindergarten classes. The Reyes twins, Camila and Elena, invited their teachers to the local flea market where their family has a booth on the weekends. The teachers view the flea market experience differently, using either a deficit lens or an anti-deficit lens. The interactions between the teachers demonstrate the value of having a critical friend who can shift the perspective to one that focuses on identifying students' strengths. The teachers went beyond just identifying the students' strengths; they also identified how those strengths could be leveraged in their classrooms. Learning about Camila and Elena's flea market vendor experiences can help their teachers create math activities in their classrooms that build the students' confidence and math learning.

We highlight the key points for consideration from the case as follows:

1. *Challenging Deficit Perspectives*

    What we see and feel tends to mirror our attitudes and thoughts. If you are noticing something negative in an experience, ask yourself why. What are you focusing on? Try identifying two positive outcomes of the experiences instead. If you need help identifying the positive outcomes, then ask a friend. Your perspective as the teacher is essential for the experiences you create for your students. Macella was a critical friend to Nina in that she continuously challenged Nina's perspective to help her see the math strengths the Reyes twins demonstrated. The work of reframing your views of language use, math learning, and even flea markets can help you see the value of students' out-of-school experiences.

Macella had an easy time trusting Camila and Elena's math knowledge with counting since she was familiar with some Spanish words. Nina was not familiar with Spanish words and doubted whether what the Reyes twins said was correct. Nina's experience might be relatable to you if your students speak a language you are not familiar with. However, trusting your students is an important aspect of seeing their math strengths. Nina could use context clues, like how the parents and customers were responding, and assume the best about the students. Assuming the best and keeping a strengths-based perspective is preferable to a deficit perspective.

2. *Math Beyond the Grade-Level Standards*

    Math content becomes easier to understand when it is put in a context that makes sense to children. In real life, children are exposed to math contexts that do not necessarily fall within a particular grade level. In this case, Nina is concerned about including money in their math lessons because it is a first-grade topic at their school. However, children know about money and most likely have seen money in some aspect. It is appropriate to use contexts that are not within a particular grade level when children have prior knowledge, and it makes sense to be used. The teachers could create word problems that include either whole dollar amounts when buying or selling items. They could even introduce dimes as a way of skip counting by tens to one hundred. The math lesson might not be approached the same way as one taught in first grade, but money should not be avoided in kindergarten just because it is found in a different grade level's standards.

3. *Leveraging Students' Lived Experiences in Math Lessons*

When students' feel a connection to their school activities, they tend to be more engaged and find more meaning in the learning. However, real-world experiences for one student might not be the same for another student. As the teacher, you will need to consider whose experiences are being used for math examples and whose experiences are not represented. If you notice there are students in your class who are disengaged or shy, it could be helpful to purposefully leverage those students' experiences. If you are worried about how the other students might connect with the context, like Nina was worried, then consider how you will bridge their knowledge of the task. You could use your students to help explain the context through a show and tell experience and then let them be the experts who help the rest of the class. Rotate these roles with new tasks so that every student can feel like their experiences outside of school are valuable and worth exploring.

Appendix

Process for Analyzing Cases Using Anti-Deficit Noticing

Step 1: Identify your own assumptions and biases about the children, families, and the math content in the case.

Step 2: Reflect on the instructional decisions the teacher took and the impact those decisions had on the students' math identities and their opportunities to engage in the math.

Step 3: Use the reflection questions and explore possible connections to your own teaching.

Step 4: Use the "Points for Consideration" to further develop anti-deficit noticing.

Step 5: Reread the case with an anti-deficit lens and reimagine opportunities that create equitable math learning experiences for all students.

References

Adiredja, A. P., & Louie, N. (2020). Untangling the web of deficit discourse in mathematics education. *For the Learning of Mathematics*, *40*(1), 42–46.

Aguirre, J. M., Mayfield-Ingram, K., & Martin, D. B. (2024). *The impact of identity in K-8 mathematics: Rethinking equity-based practices, expanded edition*. National Council of Teachers of Mathematics.

Bartell, T. G., Wager, A. A., Edwards, A. R., Battey, D., Foote, M. Q., & Spencer, J. (2017). Toward a framework for research linking equitable teaching with the Standards for Mathematical Practice. *Journal for Research in Mathematics Education*, *48*(1), 7–21. https://doi.org/10.5951/jresematheduc.48.1.0007

Gorski, P. C., & Pothini, S. G. (2024). *Case studies on diversity and social justice education* (3rd ed.). Routledge. https://doi.org/10.4324/9781351142526

Gorksi, P. C., & Swalwell, K. (2015). Equity literacy for all. *Educational Leadership*, *72*(6), 34–40.

Gutiérrez, R. (2009). Framing equity: Helping students "play the game" and "change the game." *Teaching for Excellence and Equity in Mathematics*, *1*(1), 4–8.

Hand, V. (2012). Seeing diversity: The epistemological underpinnings of mathematical learning and participation. *Review of Educational Research*, *82*(1), 103–131. https://doi.org/10.1007/978-3-319-05978-5_10

Jacobs, V. R., Lamb, L. L., & Philipp, R. A. (2010). Professional noticing of children's mathematical thinking. *Journal for Research in Mathematics Education*, *41*(2), 169–202. https://doi.org/10.5951/jresematheduc.41.2.0169

Langer-Osuna, J. M., & Esmonde, I. (2017). Identity in research on mathematics education. In J. Cai (Ed.), *Compendium for research in mathematics education* (pp. 637–648). National Council of Teachers of Mathematics.

Leonard, J., & Martin, D. B. (2013). *The brilliance of Black children in mathematics*. Information Age Publishing.

Louie, N., Adiredja, A. P., & Jessup, N. (2021). Teacher noticing from a sociopolitical perspective: The FAIR framework for anti-deficit noticing. *ZDM – Mathematics Education*, *53*, 95–107. https://doi.org/10.1007/s11858-021-01229-2

Martin, D. B., Anderson, C. R., & Shah, N. (2017). Race and mathematics education. In Cai, J. (Ed.), *Compendium for research in mathematics education* (pp. 607–636). National Council of Teachers of Mathematics.

Moldavan, A. M., & Gonzalez, M. L. (2023). Engaging preservice teachers with equity-related cases to make visible the inequities in mathematics teaching. *Action in Teacher Education*, *45*(4), 282–301. https://doi.org/10.1080/01626620.2023.2242312

Redman, G. L., & Redman, A. R. (2011). *A casebook for exploring diversity* (4th ed.). Pearson.

Rhodes, S., Moldavan, A. M., Smithey, M., & DePiro, A. (2023). Five keys for growing confident math learners. *Mathematics Teacher: Learning and Teaching PK–12*, *116*(1), 8–15. https://doi.org/10.5951/MTLT.2022.0225

Shah, N. (2019). "Asians are good at math" is not a compliment: STEM success as a threat to personhood. *Harvard Educational Review*, *89*(4), 661–686. https://doi.org/10.17763/1943-5045-89.4.661

Shah, N., & Coles, J. (2020). Preparing teachers to notice race in classrooms: Contextualizing the competencies of preservice teachers with antiracist inclinations. *Journal of Teacher Education*. https://doi.org/10.1177/0022487119900204

Sherin, M. G., Russ, R. S., & Colestock, A. A. (2011). Accessing mathematics teachers' in-the-moment noticing. In M. G. Sherin, V. R. Jacobs, & R. A. Philipp (Eds.), *Mathematics teacher noticing: Seeing through teachers' eyes* (pp. 79–94). Routledge. https://doi.org/10.4324/9780203832714

Shulman, L. (1992). Toward a pedagogy of cases. In J. H. Shulman (Ed.), *Case methods in teacher education* (pp. 1–29). Teachers College Press.

Wager, A. A. (2014). Noticing children's participation: Insights into teacher positionality toward equitable mathematics pedagogy. *Journal for Research in Mathematics Education*, *45*(3), 312–350. https://doi.org/10.5951/jresematheduc.45.3.0312

For Product Safety Concerns and Information please contact our EU
representative GPSR@taylorandfrancis.com
Taylor & Francis Verlag GmbH, Kaufingerstraße 24, 80331 München, Germany

www.ingramcontent.com/pod-product-compliance
Lightning Source LLC
Chambersburg PA
CBHW070807230426
43665CB00017B/2516